GOOD ENOUGH NOUGH NOW

JESSICA PETTITT

GOOD ENOUGH NOW

HOW DOING THE BEST WE CAN
WITH WHAT WE HAVE
IS BETTER THAN NOTHING

SOUND WISDOM
P.O. Box 310
Shippensburg, PA 17257-0310

For more information on publishing and distribution rights, call 717-530-2122 or e-mail info@ soundwisdom.com.

Quantity Sales. Special discounts are available on quantity purchases by corporations, associations, and others. For details, contact the Sales Department at Sound Wisdom.

While efforts have been made to verify information contained in this publication, neither the author nor the publisher assumes any responsibility for errors, inaccuracies, or omissions.

While this publication is chock-full of useful, practical information, it is not intended to be legal or accounting advice. All readers are advised to seek competent lawyers and accountants to follow laws and regulations that may apply to specific situations.

The reader of this publication assumes responsibility for the use of the information. The author and publisher assume no responsibility or liability whatsoever on the behalf of the reader of this publication.

ISBN 13 TP: 978-1-937879-84-6
ISBN 13 eBook: 978-1-937879-85-3

For Worldwide Distribution, Printed in the U.S.A.

Cover/Jacket designer: Eileen Rockwell
Interior designer: Terry Clifton
Graphic design by Lush Newton

Library of Congress Cataloging-in-Publication Data

Names: Pettitt, Jessica, author.
Title: Good enough now : how doing the best we can with what we have is
   better than nothing / Jessica Pettitt.
Description: Shippensburg, PA : Sound Wisdom, 2017. | Includes
   bibliographical references and index.
Identifiers: LCCN 2017005196 | ISBN 9781937879846 (paperback)
Subjects: LCSH: Self-actualization (Psychology) | Self. | Interpersonal
   relations. | Teams in the workplace. | BISAC: SELF-HELP / Personal Growth
   / Success. | SELF-HELP / Motivational & Inspirational.
Classification: LCC BF637.S4 P4484 2017 | DDC 158.1--dc23
LC record available at https://lccn.loc.gov/2017005196

1 2 3 4 5 6 7 8 / 20 19 18 17

"The role of the artist is exactly the same as the role of the lover. If I love you, I have to make you conscious of the things you don't see."
—JAMES BALDWIN

This book is dedicated to every teacher, instructor, and trainer out there who is trying and showing up as a parent, mentor, and educator to validate and witness those who don't have the strength to do it themselves.

Thank you, Dr. Jennings, for leading the way.

CONTENTS

FOREWORD

One of my heroes is the tragically unknown and under-appreciated Bayard Rustin, and one of my favorite things that he said was that, "We need in every community a group of angelic troublemakers." Jessica Pettitt is one such angelic troublemaker, and she has written a book which will help you become one as well.

I have been involved in diversity and inclusion work for over a decade now and there is still, in 2017, a very strong tendency for people to see this work as a sort of intellectual endeavor; the idea that being inclusive is simply a matter of being one of those that "gets it." This is how we continue to have organizations, institutions, industries, and communities that take great pride in, and make great noise about, their wonderfully inclusive intentions, yet are not actually inclusive. Talking the talk rather than walking the walk. And let's be honest, the talking is a lot easier. We write poetic declarations of commitment to diversity and inclusion, post them on our websites, addend them to our annual reports and give ourselves humanitarian awards. We too easily and too frequently convince ourselves that if we are just "good people" with good intentions that inclusion is the automatic result.

Inclusion is no more an intellectual endeavor than fitness is. While a good many of us have tried to think, talk and intend our way to fitness, the reality remains that it requires getting out of bed and going to the gym. It requires effort, action, and a bit of discomfort.

While *getting it* is certainly a part of the journey, there is no inclusion without *doing it* and that is what this book is about. Inclusion is inherently activist, and if you are ready to act you are looking in the right place.

As people go, Jessica Pettitt is one of the better ones I have come across. Her intentions are the best. Yet, as you will read in the pages ahead, she has made mistakes. Good intentions notwithstanding, she has not known what to do at times. She has, at times, not understood people, things and situations.

In this book, Jessica has courageously harvested loads of valuable stuff from the experiences of those around her, from the people she has reached through her work, from the insights and experiences of others, but especially from her own life. Which is a big part of what makes this such an accessible, honest, and actionable message.

Often when we consider big, complex issues such as diversity, inclusion, equality, and justice we assume that our actions must be big and complex as well; marches, protests, social movements, and policy initiatives come to mind. These kinds of efforts have proven integral to progress in this country and others and will likely always have their place, but they can cast a great shadow over the smaller things of equal importance like the "party-of-one" work that Jessica speaks of in the pages ahead.

A long, long time ago I served in the United States Marine Corps as an infantryman. We learned in bootcamp that one of our most important skills was land navigation; the ability to figure out where you are, where you are going, and to get there, regardless of terrain, weather, etc. I traveled a great deal during my time as a Marine and had the opportunity to navigate in just about every type of terrain imaginable, and even ended up teaching land navigation for about 6 months in Okinawa, Japan. I came to consider my compass (which I still have) one of my most important tools and took great pride in my ability to use it with great efficiency and accuracy.

You hold in your hands a compass. Use it. The stakes are high. Be good to each other. And stop for the tater-tots.

Joe Gerstandt

http://www.joegerstandt.com/

The Value of Difference

INTRODUCTION

We make excuses when we focus on what we cannot control instead of focusing on what we can control. *Good Enough Now* is going to help us change our focus.

This book excites me. It excites me because I know that it will help me and others be able to look at ourselves, learn about ourselves and position us to do things that we may never have thought possible. We will be able to have better conversations with others, determine responsibilities to take on, be more accountable to ourselves and others, and ultimately discover that our best self already exists and is ready to press into action. Ultimately, we will eliminate the excuses we give when talking about why our relationships aren't as good as they could be, why we don't achieve what we think we should, and why our conversations don't go as deep as we would like.

It is through truth and understanding that we can position ourselves to have the more difficult and meaningful conversations, build better relationships, and be accountable to the people around us.

Jessica tells her truth. She doesn't hold back. She shares more about herself then most of my good friends would share with me. Not only will you get to know Jessica, but through her eyes you will expand how you see the people around you. Most importantly, you will gain a better understanding of how you see yourself.

Jessica teaches us not to let our past experiences—even the negative ones—hold us back, but rather how to use those experiences to uncover more about ourselves and be positioned to drive forward, now.

Most people know more than they need to in order to be successful in their relationships, their jobs, and as members of their communities. *Good Enough Now* will help you do what we all need to do, and that is to put all of that knowledge into action.

We need to move forward. Nothing happens in the status quo. It is only by taking chances, exploring outside of our personal universe and putting into action the knowledge that we possess that we discover our best self, and we are able to unleash the enormous potential that we all have.

Our accountability to ourselves and to the people around us demands that we take these steps, and *Good Enough Now* enables us to do so. Accountability cannot exist without honesty. The key is that honesty must truly start with us. We must be honest with ourselves with regards to our abilities and desires and then unleash that personal honesty in the form of positive action.

Jessica, through her experiences and unabashed willingness to share those experiences, is the perfect person to lead us on this journey. It is exciting, a little scary, and critically important that we drive forward as our very best awaits us as we truly are *Good Enough Now*!

Sam Silverstein
Author: *No More Excuses* & *Non-Negotiable*
Past President, National Speakers Association

PROLOGUE

When reading this particular book, which question comes up for you first?

The Head Question

Why am I reading this? What is the point? Why does it matter to matter?

The Heart Question

How will this book change my life? How does this all matter?

The Action Question

Let's talk bottom line—how will this make me money? Make a difference that lasts? What do I do and where do I start?

All of these questions are important.

If I handed you a Magic 8-Ball and you were to ask your burning question, you would get one of the twenty answers that preexists on the dice inside the mysterious blue liquid. Before I introduce the Good Enough Now method, the Magic 8-Ball metaphor works because there are nine answers that preexist in each of us no matter the question. Head, Heart, Action. Head, Action, Heart. Heart, Action, Head. These are the three most common response patterns used in the Good Enough Now model.

Head   **Heart**   **Action**

You gravitate to one type of question more than the others, or you dismiss one type of question more than others. This is pretty typical behavior. Congratulations, you are typical!

Like the dice inside of a Magic 8-Ball, the options of answers are all inside and don't change. All three of these variables— Head-, Heart-, and Action-oriented responses—exist inside of all of us. We typically weigh one (maybe two) over the other(s), but they never go away.

I will answer all of these questions and more in all three manners throughout the book by using data (Head), reflection questions (Heart), and activities (Action). Take notice when you seem to connect with one manner over another or find yourself skimming or skipping over different sections.

These icons will mark sections that are written specifically to appeal to one variable over another. One variable isn't better or more problematic than the other, nor is one more important than another.

To begin, we must first understand the model and apply it to ourselves. For instance, we can put it to the test by looking at how the model relates to other people who do nothing, it seems, but frustrate us and stall our progress, miss the point, or just seem not to care. Lastly, this model dictates not just our behaviors but guides us to roll out significantly more successful campaigns, initiatives, and connections leading to an increase in loyalty, retention, innovation, and inclusion.

I promise.

Why It Matters to Matter

Bottom line—it does. It matters not just to future generations but to those less fortunate than you and to you.

I learned that it matters to matter while doing consulting work for a major automobile brand. While working at different dealerships, I would conduct focus groups with the different "levels" of employees—mechanics, administrative, sales, and leadership. My job was to review employee engagement survey results across departments as compared to the average of all dealerships and facilitate a conversation of ways to encourage more engagement practices within the existing culture, budget, time, and space limitations.

At this one dealership, I discovered that two employees had similar negative stories being told about them, though they worked in totally different departments. It seems that one of the top performing mechanics and a favorite floor supervisor had become lazy, tired, and less connected, with the other employees. There was no overlap in the circles of these two employees, but both seemed to take longer lunches, leave early, and arrive late. They both at one time were seen as the biggest team players. Then, suddenly, they were seen as just the opposite. I spoke with both of these men individually to see if they recognized any behavior pattern changes, and both confidentially informed me that they were going through chemotherapy and didn't want anyone at work to know or people would think they were sick, tired, lazy, or not a team player anymore. This crushed me. I asked each of them if I could confidentially set up a meeting with their supervisors to see how the dealership could best support them. The next month, the owner reached out to me and thanked me. By setting up a ride share program and food delivery system, all of the employees were working together again. It matters to have everyone be able to show up fully and support one another fully. Moreover, it matters to feel seen and a part of a team. When space was provided for the truth, engagement at that dealership increased, as did the quality of life for the employees.

New, unknown, or inaccurate information in our stories about ourself and others, limits our ability to be engaged, create, support, and retain those around us. We work so hard on the relationships that we have and can self-sabotage them, conspicuously or unconsciously, by limiting who and how we are. We also ask others to change to make us more comfortable. Kenji Yoshino, Professor of Constitutional Law at NYU, shares the concept of "covering," which addresses this hiding or self-limiting that occurs to make others comfortable. In the March 2014 *Harvard Business Review*, Yoshino and Christie Smith, Managing Principal of DeLoitte University Leadership Center for Inclusion, wrote an article titled "Fear of Being Different Stifles Talent" after surveying "some 3,000 employees in more than 20 large US firms... spanning 10 industries [that] stated [an] emphasis on inclusiveness" (Yoshino & Smith, 2). Their study found:

- 29% altered their attire, grooming, or mannerisms to make their identity less obvious.

- 40% refrained from behavior commonly associated with a given identity.

- 57% avoided sticking up for their identity group.

- 18% limited contact with members of a group they belong to.

- 61% of survey participants said they had faced overt or implicit pressure to cover in some way or to downplay their difference from the mainstream.

- 66% of these employees said that it significantly undermined their sense of self.

- 50% state that it diminished their sense of commitment.

- 51% perceived demands [to cover] from leadership that affected their view of opportunities with the organization.

Although covering was more prevalent among traditionally underrepresented groups, including gays (83%), blacks (79%), women (66%), Hispanics (63%), and Asians (61%), [the authors] found a surprising incidence among straight white men, 45% of whom [reported] they downplayed characteristics such as age, physical disabilities, and mental health issues (Ibid.).

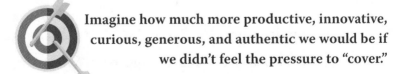 **Imagine how much more productive, innovative, curious, generous, and authentic we would be if we didn't feel the pressure to "cover."**

What would happen if we worked to diminish the instances where we consciously or unconsciously made others feel that they had to hide, adjust, limit, or lie about an important piece of who they are in our presence? The amount of time and energy used to hide limits our ability to engage, connect, share, and thrive confidently. "Covering" is both internal and external. We can hide from ourselves as well as others.

If we can first know *who* and *how* we show up in relation to others, we can do something with this knowledge. If we can consciously reflect on a time when we had to hide or cover, we can have empathy for others doing the same thing. Then and only then can we show up fully in all of our strengths and weaknesses and vulnerably depend on one another. Instead of spending time and treasure to appear a certain way or strategically associating with certain people and not others—we can just be. We could worry less about self-fulfilling prophecies of stereotypes and rumor mills like the dealership employees going through chemo. We can advocate for each other when something difficult or uncomfortable occurs. An appreciation for how we show up to others sets the stage for our full selves to fully connect with others more successfully and consistently.

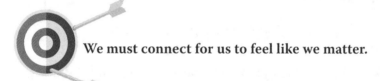 We must connect for us to feel like we matter.

How to Matter

Excellent! Perfect! 100 percent! (Compared to everyone else!)

Perhaps it is because I am a Virgo or a Myers-Briggs type ENTJ or a white woman from the South; I don't know the source, but these elements of expectation have ruled the greater portion of my life.

A cloud of disappointment still hovers over me for every time I did less than perfect. (Let's not even talk about when I had to drop out of Calculus.) Letters of reprimand and "resignation" float in and out of focus in my anxiety-ridden memories. Regrets, failures, and personal struggles fuel self-doubt, self-limiting beliefs, and habitual excuses. My whole life, or my lived experience, has brought me to who and how I am today.

Perhaps you can identify.

These experiences seem to surface just in time for a new opportunity, big decision, upcoming adventure, or confrontation and leave me (perhaps us) feeling inadequate, underprepared, irrelevant, meaningless, and not worthy.

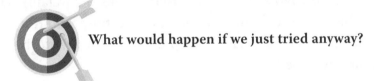 **What would happen if we just tried anyway?**

My grandmother used to say, "Ask and you have a 50 percent chance of getting a different answer than *no*." You start with "no" for an answer; asking can get you a "yes." There are many reasons why we don't ask or try. Most of these patterns are rooted in our own history of failures, embarrassing attempts, personal fear, lack of preparation, and a missing sense of safety. We can predict an outcome, but we can't *know* the outcome until we try.

To add to the reality of this struggle, we often are navigating our lives with limited resources, time shortages, stressful situations, difficult people, taboo topics, and complicated personal narratives about who and how we are to be. For some, showing up is an act of revolution, while others seem to float through life without struggle or challenge. The truth is that all of these individuals—yes, even you, and double yes, even the hurtful or annoying people in your life—matter.

Often the concept of "coexisting" is thrown around as something to aspire to, but the truth is that we already do. We just haven't taken the time to notice before. Navel-gazing, self-absorption, fear of failure, and worse, the fear of offending someone prevent us from living in our own coexistence. When we do pay attention, we quickly make a judgment about the scenario based on the assumptions we have consciously or unconsciously learned throughout life. These judgments and assumptions do two things: 1) keep us safe, and 2) help us prepare for what is ahead of us.

After years of diversity and communication trainings, I am here to reclaim my judgments and assumptions. You can, too. It isn't about *making* them that may need editing, it is *what we do with the ones we make* that we need to claim our responsibly. Once we understand who and how we are in the world, we can decide what to keep and what needs to be worked on or developed.

I posit that instead of striving for perfect, we collectively take responsibility for who and how we are in the world. This is a *huge* first step, but it is imperative. Once we know what others already know about us, we can then pay attention to others more fully. We can engage in conversations that we may feel uncomfortable with and really listen to the other person.

This process isn't about *never* making judgments or assumptions, but recognizing we all do. To feel prepared or safe isn't a bad thing. If a moral judgment needed to be handed down, it would be on the *responses* or behavior patterns related to these judgments and assumptions that we don't even notice and/or claim no responsibility for in the first place.

We make judgments and assumptions when we parallel park, pick a seat in a crowded room, ask someone out for a date, vote, approach someone with a concern, and every time we ask a question of another person. With each question or situation, we think we know what is going to happen next. We might be right. We might be wrong. Regardless, we have a script of some sort about the scenario that we play out in our minds. This script plays over and over again and can limit as well as create a sense of possibility. The script can affect our self-talk as well as our interactions with others. The key is the *possibility* of *possibility*.

I am not suggesting never making judgments or assumptions, but using these stories to print a draft of a story instead of a final edition. By printing a draft, I mean spacing the concepts out, triple-spaced with extra-wide margins so that you can anticipate edits. Print a draft of a story instead of the final edition as you are engaging with someone. Anticipating edits implies that your story can get better, more accurate, or change altogether. Do you want to know what the most courageous, giving, daring, and vulnerable act that you can do is? Enter into a dialogue with someone with room for edits. Entertain a genuine curiosity about the other person. Consider the potential of where the conversation could go. Leave room for edits for your own growth and learning.

It is generally habitual to grasp tightly to our stories informed by our conscious and unconscious lived experiences and force others to comply. When others throw us for a loop, we are surprised with something unexpectedly delightful; then tragedy strikes and the unknown becomes known. We quickly make sense of the unexpected instead of staying open and learning new information, consciously acquiring a new experience or new content. We will often write a significantly more complicated addition to our existing story to make something make "sense" instead of being wrong. Look at any given conspiracy theory for evidence of how complicated making sense can get when we could just admit we didn't know something.

Being right is often thought of as the best method of living, but it comes with its own struggles too. Is being right what matters most in life, or is making a difference more important? Is never failing more important, or editing and learning as we go? Power, privilege, and high expectations can feel overwhelming and often unattainable. Instead of competing for more or opting out due to fear of failure, I propose that being good enough is what matters as a starting place. We can get better, but we have to launch from somewhere. We are good enough now.

A friend questioned the concept of good enough, arguing that if "good enough" kicks in, there would be no innovation. Good Enough Now is the starting place, not the resting place. My contrarian friend talked about how new iPhones would not be better without updates and new bells and whistles. This is true. Just the other day on a dog walk, my partner, Loren, and I talked about Volkswagen coming out with an electric van. Neither of us are early adopters[1]—we don't own a microwave—so we both agreed to look at the vans in their third or fourth iterations so that a lot of the problems would be worked out and the price would be lower. We are anticipating future models. However, the designers of the new Volkswagen electric van at some point determine that the van is good enough to begin manufacturing. This level of good enough has to meet safety standards. While there may be problems that become apparent after release or even recalls, at least the first model was released. It was good enough. History is full of examples of this concept. The first automobile didn't have brakes. Now they have multiple gears, computers, and some have fish tanks! Good enough isn't about perfect—it is dependent on the possibility of the unknown while operating with what is currently known.

---

1   I first learned the term "early adopters" from Rogers's Innovation Curve. The other counterparts to this model are the "laggards" on the other end.

Releasing something into the world for judgments is exhilarating and terrifying until it becomes comfortable and a habit.

Every time we engage in a conversation with another person, we have the opportunity to utilize the *good enough* idea—we think we know how a conversation is going to go but are open to it (possibly) going in different directions. Whether it is a stranger or a conversation about a difficult topic, we can stand in the idea that we—and they—are good enough now. We can leave room for edits with our judgments and preconceived ideas. We can remain open to possibility. We can be curious. We can be responsible for how and who we are in all of our interactions with strangers, dear friends, family, co-workers, and children.

We do so believing that what we have to offer is beneficial to others and that this matters. Most of us don't design Volkswagen vans, but we engage in conversations with clerks, co-workers, friends, and family. These conversations are not typically scripted and staged in advance for maximum impact. Some people or topics are avoided because we feel that the "risk" of doing something wrong, offensive, or unintended isn't worth the effort. Others avoid us as well. The stories that lead to personal engagement or avoidance are our responsibility. Noting that we write these stories about others and ourselves is how judgments and assumptions are made, and they are safe because we are used to them. These same patterns reappear over and over again and give us the illusion of being prepared.

Good enough isn't about perfect—it is dependent on possibility of the unknown while operating with what is currently known. Together we will reclaim responsibility for what we believe we know and the accompanying habits while also leaving space for what is possible.

This is how to matter.

What Do I Do? Where to Start?

Inclined to leap first and ask questions later?

There isn't a pill (that I know of) that fixes everything all at once. No matter what you see in commercials, the way to lose weight and keep it off is to burn more calories than you ingest forever. This is a lifestyle, not an immersion experience. And like any time that I take on a new exercise regimen (again), you have to break it down into tiny steps and, when making some progress, keep challenging yourself. Trust me, my annual habit of walking a half marathon doesn't actually make up the year's worth of exercise, even though it takes four and half hours. (This equals five minutes a week if it did count for the year, so I am going to need to work out *way* more than this anyway.) I just keep telling myself I am faster than a person sitting on the couch. (The key is to not be sitting in my desk chair when I say it.) Swiveling, though fun, doesn't count as exercise. You can't cram self-work into an intensive focused weekend and be done with it—it takes time and is repeated often and always.

The first step in (re)claiming responsibility for our response patterns is to understand the stories we write. Once we have a better understanding of *who* and *how* we are in the world, we can determine which patterns we value in ourselves and keep them! There will be other patterns that seem incongruent with our core values or preferences. Studying our patterns is excellent self-awareness, and you can then do one of two things: 1) keep the patterns, or 2) work on changing. There will also be patterns that you don't like about yourself, and this is where your self-work can begin. Don't throw the baby out with the bathwater. Keep the good stuff. Keep the complicated stuff if you like it. Focus on what you are most interested in changing.

When determining what to do, how to fix something, or what actions need to be taken, it is important to start with the fact that we write stories as *the truth* first. The content of the stories is based on our lived experiences, habits, and the like. This content can also be derived from unconscious bias, positive or negative; it can be correct or inaccurate, important or irrelevant, and all of it is our individual responsibility. We are responsible for what limits our own connections with others. Whether we like it or not, connections with others are imperative to facilitate relationships and simple interactions with other people. These connections are also how we build better teams, work together better, and even encourage innovation, creative ideas, learning, application of new techniques or procedures, etc.

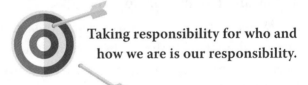

Taking responsibility for who and how we are is our responsibility.

We cannot successfully ask for someone else to do anything for us if we haven't done the work too. By doing our own self-reflection work, we can then ask others to take responsibility for their own responses. Moreover, once we take note of our own behavior patterns, we can keep the ones we like and focus on the ones we don't instead of feeling stuck or overwhelmed. As we get better with ourselves, we will become better with others. Once we are more aware of our own way of showing up, we can also use this knowledge to intentionally seek out those different from ourselves to make us stronger. Learning, listening, communicating in a more conscious and authentic manner will in fact build strong, loyal, and generous interactions with others based on genuine curiosity. These strong connections can mutually support the common connection in a positive, vulnerable, and real way.

Self-awareness work is all about the narrative draft. The story we tell ourselves, show others, and others read about us could be completely different from each other, but hopefully they are pretty close together. The closer these stories are to each other, the more authentically you are living this life. The more authentically you can show up, the more you will inspire others to be their fullest self. This leads directly to better conversations and relationships no matter if you are at the grocery store discussing cantaloupes in passing with a stranger or working through a life-changing moment with your closest support network. These life-changing moments, or crucible moments, change your life, connections, and purpose. It is here—in the empty space, the margins, or the white space between lines on your draft—that the meaning of life can appear.

When I stop in to a Starbucks at an airport, I know that I may never interact with the barista again. I can make the brief interaction the highlight of their day, or I can just be another person. Personally, I like making people smile or even laugh; it makes me enjoy my day better. Those standing in line behind me may or may not be paying attention; if they are, they may be annoyed at the few extra seconds I take to make a connection. At least they know me as someone who makes connections. Making connections is an important value for me. The barista may also be annoyed at the extra time I take, but it is totally worth it to me that for three seconds during that shift they existed in my life; I saw them. Sure, maybe this is how I get an extra pack of dried fruit for my oatmeal cup without asking for it. We really win because we connected.

This connection with one another is all that we have that *really matters,* so do what you need to do to connect. My roommate from college works as a psychologist in a hospice care center. She talks with dying people about *what matters.* The answer is always *connections*—not belongings, achievements, mistakes, or failures, but connections. We must be connected with ourself to truly and powerfully connect with someone else, even if it is for a short period of time with a random barista or raising a child or launching a new product line or pulling together after a crisis to survive. We must connect. How we connect starts with how we habitually respond or show up with others. What we do with this connection varies widely. Others also connect with us as mentors, supervisors, teammates, strangers seeking assistance, and people passing us on the sidewalk.

SECTION ONE

GOOD

As I developed this Head, Heart, Action model, I began to see it everywhere. When talking about long-lasting, deep connections, I see a practical application of how people respond to situations that fits right in line with the model. My former college roommate, now a clinical psychologist, often shares with me life lessons she takes from her clients. At one point, she was working with patients in hospice care, and she got in the habit of asking her long-time married patients for the "secret." As she shared the responses, I easily sorted them into the three categories, Head, Heart, and Action.

What leads to long-lasting, deep connections?

One group spoke of routine and quantity of time spent connecting with the other. These intentional and frequent connections are regularly scheduled, held regardless of other opportunities, and become intentional and habit-forming ways of living connected. Connecting isn't an accident but a way of interacting with others as well as ourselves. Staying connected to our own sense of self allows our full self to connect to another.

These answers are more *Head* or quantifiable, planned, routine, and scheduled.

A second group of responses speaks to something larger—not just a self-connection or a personal relationship as much as a duty or calling to the larger world. Connections are how we, as humans, share energy with one another, shift energy in a space, and manifest an environment where all can feel connected if not included. On an even bigger scale, others see genuine connections and try to follow suit, leading to more meaningful connections with others. Once a person has felt included there is no going back, and you want to bring others into the group for even more connections. This becomes an expectation, a regular occurrence, or even a habit.

These responses are connected to something larger than just the two people connecting and are more *Heart*.

Lastly, the responses were funny, off topic, and powerful examples of humor, personality, and connection. Picking your battles, listening, learning when to shut up, and letting the other person act like they won. These kinds of responses are better in the long run but happen in the moment. My favorite one my roommate shared with me is, "Don't have a gun in the house."

Action-oriented responses range from doing nothing to doing something together.

Take Notice

What to do and where to start is here. One of these three response patterns resonates with you. You get one of them hands down. Maybe you can identify with two of them. Perhaps one is totally out of your realm of understanding. The place to start is to recognize that all three of these categories are valid types of responses. If the question were to change, it is possible that you would respond differently. You (and I) are responsible for how we respond, what we understand, as well as what we don't quite get. It isn't that one of these response patterns is right and the others are wrong; all are accurate answers from the folks who were responding to the question. We tend to show up in *our* particular way. We can, however, become understanding of the *other* ways. Moreover, others in our lives show up in their way. It is advantageous to understand their way. It is also very real to recognize that these other people are generally more aware of how we show up than we are conscious of or deliberately choosing to.

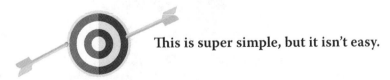 This is super simple, but it isn't easy.

Noticing that how we respond and habitually show up in our connections is the first step in breaking down barriers, writing more accurate stories about ourselves and others, and (re)claiming responsibility for what we unconsciously do or don't do. Notice. Pay attention. Start here. This is what to do.

As you begin to notice your own behavior patterns, try not to make judgments about these responses or lack thereof. These are your patterns.

Some of the patterns you will notice that you like. *Great!* Keep those. Some of the patterns you will not like. *Great!* Work on those. Some of the patterns you will notice are incongruent with other patterns or your personal values and that may just be the case; at least you now know about the inconsistencies. Others you won't understand at all. It is hard to categorize what you don't notice or understand. So ask your best friend. If they think you are ready, they will tell you. They know you better than you do. Once you know which patterns you want to focus on, the real work starts.

Nonahedron

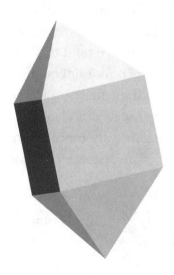

Like the Magic 8-Ball, Head-, Heart-, and Action-based responses (or lack thereof) lay within each of us. A nonahedron is a nine-sided figure—it is what our "dice" would look like no matter what question we pose or situation we inhabit. No matter our response, all three variables are present. Our go-to response pattern is made up of one or two of the variables. The third variable is still present and can be used to create excuses or power our way through the situation. No matter what, all three are present.

If you think of the Head, Heart, and Action responses as sides of a nonahedron-shaped dice, they would look like this:[2]

2   These dice were designed by David Bachman through Shapeways.com. He can be contacted at bachman@pitzer.edu.

Every time something happens, you roll your dice and respond with a combination of Head, Heart, and Action. Each side of the nonahedron has one primary response, but the other two are also present on either side. This informs the way you respond.

 Take notice.

Your nonahedron dice might be weighted to always land the same way over and over again. Even though this is predictable, you may not be aware of this pattern. Others can often share this information with you—it is just up to you to believe them. As you notice your responses and behavior patterns you will be able to remove the weight and roll freely. This sense of flexibility will allow you to do more with the resources you already have and build on the relationships to which you have already connected. As you increase your endurance and flexibility, you can even begin to apply this to new situations, people, and circumstances; but let's not get ahead of ourselves.

The meaning or reasoning behind a behavior pattern is important to know, and taking responsibility for the pattern of behavior means that you are uncovering the root of the behavior. These roots are directly connected to your life experiences, identities, as well as the life-changing or crucible moments that have forever altered your conscious and unconscious connections with others. (Re)claiming responsibility and offering forgiveness to yourself and others, and being able to accept your own strengths and weaknesses is hard work. This is where we must release our expectations of perfection and do the best we can with what we have some of the time. This is where we begin to accept ourself and others, familiar and strange, as we currently are.

It matters, and this is how to be *good enough now*.

CHAPTER
1

START WITH A PARTY OF ONE

"Alvarez party of five." "Jill party of two." "McMillian reunion party, right this way."

I waited tables throughout college and graduate school. No matter your shift or duties for that shift, at some point you host guests, keep a waiting list, and escort customers to their table. Even if you haven't ever waited tables before, when you go to a restaurant you have to leave your name and the number of people in your party. As tables become available, you get one in order of preferences and arrival. This is also when you specify the number of children in your group or party, inside or out seating, smoking or non, or no preference—just first available. When dining alone, you are a party of one.

Being a party of one at a restaurant can be awkward or delightful or something in between. Keith Ferrazzi and Tahl Raz wrote *Never Eat Alone: And Other Secrets to Success, One Relationship at a Time* in 2014. It received great reviews and built a movement. This isn't really what I am referencing here. Think about the last time you were on a road trip by yourself or maybe an errand day and you pulled over to take a break. For me, this is usually a hole-in-the-wall place that looks like it will have tater tots. Let's be honest—I pull over for tater tots no matter what. When I am eating by myself, I can read the local magazines, eavesdrop on neighboring conversations, check in on Facebook, or just enjoy a moment alone. I try to clear my mind with each sip of a milkshake. By the end of a meal alone, I am ready to conquer the next errand on my to-do list or the next several hours of road on my trip. Being alone, still, present, and conscious, I can then refresh myself.

"Party of one" is the language I use to focus the scope of responsibility work on the individual level. For the record, there are a great number of *systems* at play when talking about how and why our society is set up the way that it is. These multiple systems are deeply flawed and I find that doing party-of-one work enables me to keep up momentum and take note of progress in real time. Several things tend to come up when I say "party of one," and it is usually not individual-based. Systems-level work, or work with or on other people, is important and has its time and place. We will go into more detail on this in the next chapter. I tend to feel overwhelmed by big picture, macro-level, and systems-level work as it is too abstract for me to tackle all at once. Focusing on other people, groups, etc., can also be fun and motivating, but ultimately I can't make anyone do anything. I promise we will get to "them," but until then let's do our own party-of-one work. When reclaiming (or, for some, taking for the first time) responsibility for our behavior patterns, we need a structure to process with. Who and how we are shows up in patterned ways, and we are responsible for these habits whether we like it or not.

Sometimes it is hard to even make ourselves do something that we need to do. Dusting comes to mind. As I have been writing this book, people keep telling me that a writer's house is the cleanest house on the block—because we can't make ourselves write. We can't make others do anything. We rarely can make ourselves do something. I can't count the number of times that I have watched a workout video while eating cheese puffs. (For the record, I make sure to alternate hands so as to not favor one over the other, as if I am doing bicep curls.) It is important that we think about and work with the full complexity of difficult issues. I believe it is also important that we build momentum and make some progress so that we continue doing the work to build better connections. Luckily, we are a pretty self-absorbed society, so let's utilize what we are good at and start with our own conscious and unconscious response and behavior patterns that result from the judgment and assumptions we already make.

If along the way of doing this party-of-one work you want to check in with someone, try your best friend. Some of us have multiple best friends, and that is awesome. Each best friend knows different bits and pieces about you or shares a different history or context with you. This is, by the way, why weddings are terrifying—too many best friends in one place, with alcohol usually being served. That is a lot of secrets, truth, and stories on one dance floor! In case you are worried that your best friend doesn't somehow qualify to help you through this process, keep this vignette in mind.

There is something your best friend does over and over again that is really annoying and you like them anyway, right? For example, the last time your best friend dated someone you didn't approve of, were you right? Of course you were and are right! You recognize these frustrating patterns of their behavior and like them anyway. The ugly truth is your best friend does this to you too. There is something that you don't know you do and they like you anyway. As you are doing party-of-one work, you can check in with your best friend like an accountability buddy, and if they think you are ready to deal with the truth they will tell you. If not, they might do what my best friend does when I can't handle the truth—take me out for ice cream. There really is no losing here. We will get to understanding *other* people, but I want to start with our *own* understanding of who and how we show up in our relationships. The process of being Good Enough Now will also ultimately help you better understand your best friends too, so they can warm up to the process by helping you through the initial party-of-one work.

> To truly reclaim responsibility for our own responses and behavior patterns, we have to start with some structure.

Party-of-one work starts with understanding how we typically show up inside of a model or paradigm, and in this case we will focus on our Head, Heart, and Action responses or lack thereof. Remember, these three variables are currently present in each of us, and it is up to us to identify how we utilize them when making connections with others. One variable isn't better than another. We do tend to respond in patterned ways that utilize one or maybe two of the variables with regularity while also fairly commonly avoiding at least one of them, but all three are there. When in doubt, check in with your best friend. You can even use the following graffiti example to demonstrate the difference between the three variables.

When you come across a new piece of graffiti, street art, or unauthorized mural, typical responses would be:

1. Why would someone devalue property and violate a city ordinance? (Head)

2. How stunning and beautiful! The community will love this. (Heart)

3. How did they get up there? (Action)

Ask yourself or your best friend—when presented with some kind of scenario, difficult topic, or unexpected conversation and you respond (or roll the dice), do you uncover a pattern of behavior? This pattern may weigh your dice so that every time, no matter what, you begin to respond in very similar patterns. Responding similarly every time can make you predictable to others. No judgment here, not a good or a bad thing, just limiting your response options out of habit. Eventually, it is possible that these habits will also cloud your perspective and lead to assumptions that everyone responds your way. This limits your ability to connect with others who are different from you. Also not necessarily a good or bad thing, but often is an unconscious outcome of our responses. We can become conscious of these limitations. Once made aware, we can opt to keep or edit our responses so that we get the outcome we are wanting. Once conscious of these patterns, we can intentionally behave, respond, and connect with others in a genuinely curious manner. These are the connections that really matter.

It is true that you may show up differently at work than you do at home, much like you might behave differently on a first date or a job interview than you do on a lazy Sunday with your closest friends or when teaching someone a new task. Overall, I have found that we all have two "go-to" behaviors that others can witness and one "go-to" behavior that runs our life. Others witness how we show up better than we can even notice. As I have done my own party-of-one work, I have uncovered that I consistently respond from an Action place first. People who know me well have to preface discussions with, "Don't do anything; we are just talking here." My partner, Loren, isn't a big consumer and would make an offhanded comment about wishing he had a lamp for his office or a new weed wacker, and within a week a new one would be in the house. This was astonishing to him, and he too had to learn a preface to deal with my typical Action response. He now says, "Please don't put this on a to-do list; this is just an idea I had." Others have to adjust their conversations with me to accommodate my responses—largely because I wasn't even aware that this was my response and it wasn't what they wanted. I would then be disappointed in their reaction to me getting things done or fixing problems for them. It was a vicious cycle until I noticed, asked clarifying questions, and adjusted my response.

Sometimes, I would ask clients or workshop participants during a side conversation, "Do you want me to be in listening mode or problem-solving mode?" This, ultimately, was a weird thing to ask—why would someone have a conversation with me and choose for me *not* to be in listening mode? So I altered my clarifying question to, "Are you looking for solutions or sharing with me?" This has a much better reaction, and I am clear as to the response that is required of me. This is still an Action response, but an Action response that fits the actual conversation so that the parties and I can truly connect. This matters. Notice, I don't have to hide my Action responses; I am just responsible for this being an appropriate response to what is warranted with this connection. Like my father used to say, "If you want to get something done, ask a Pettitt to do it." Like father like daughter.

I have also noticed that I can respond from a Head place. This response I notice more as a limitation or a place where I get stuck. Often, in the middle of a meeting or discussion I can get stuck on a detail or an unknown fact that may or may not be directly related to the conversation at hand, and I *must* get that detail figured out to move on. When collaborating with a new organization, I must have interrupted a planning meeting five times to remind the group that we needed to gather the e-mail addresses for all of the participants for marketing purposes and to follow up after the training. My counterparts would look at me and just move the conversation back to the planning session. Finally, one of my colleagues turned and said, "Jessica, we will get the e-mail addresses from the registration information." I was fine and was able to move on with the conversation. I can't imagine the exasperation that my stuck-ness on specific details causes. I guess it is similar to how I feel during training when a participant asks for specific statistics on the number of people with a certain identity and the likelihood of them interacting with one or more of this demographic. I really can't roll my eyes (look, an Action response!) at this because I am this person all the time. I am also the person on a larger national board of directors whom people turn to when they need to know the exact policy or by-law wording being referenced in a particular proposal or discussion. Head responses can be annoying and efficient, often even at the same time.

As I have stated, all three variables are in each of us. Heart responses tend to rarely be my first line of response. I have Heart responses; I am capable of Heart responses, but it isn't my go-to habitual response pattern. Heart responses and behavior patterns are definitely what I call my *third rail*. Third-rail variables will be discussed in more detail a little later. Most recently, I had a Heart response regarding the same organization I referenced a moment ago for which I serve as a national board member. After an event hosted by this organization, a few of my colleagues sat down for lunch while awaiting the airport shuttle. After sharing our perspectives and personal learning moments from the conference, a man approached and asked to join us for lunch. Upon joining us, the new lunchmate began bad-mouthing the organization with slurs, misinformation, and disdain. I was stunned and found his words to be disrespectful of me, my lunchmates, and the multiple thousands of members of the organization. I attempted to give him more accurate information to correct his comments (Head and Action) and he responded with more ego and even more disrespect. Before I knew it, I calmly explained how what he was saying was hurtful to me, those at the table, in the hotel, and members he has never met. He tried to interrupt me, and I advised him to listen to me as what I was sharing was also about him respecting himself, his membership, and this community. Swiftly, the negative energy that he brought to the table was replaced with a sense of camaraderie and connection that we all have to the mission of the larger organization.

> **Head, Heart, and Action are at our disposal if not already automatically in play when we engage in a situation, conversation, or opportunity to make a connection.**

Our mutual purpose to build a better world full of authentic connections and conversations is a mission, if not a movement, and it started right there, right then, with that lunch. My lunchmates practically applauded me and quickly dismissed his rebuttal and advised him to really listen and take in what I was saying. The lunch was wrapping up prior to this man's arrival, we all paid our bills, and as we rolled our luggage to the hotel lobby, I began to shake. It took me hours to calm down. I hadn't been that angered in ages. Furthermore, I hadn't realized how important this organization had become to me, nor how protective of this community I am. I couldn't remember anything that I had said, but I knew I deeply believed whatever it was that I said. My lunchmates still refer to that Heart response as "The Lunch." I got nervous, because I couldn't recall what I said, that I may have misrepresented the organization or myself and then began to feel the weight of being a board member and got really concerned (also a Heart response). A dear friend who was there affirmed that my response was so genuine and heartfelt that I served my leadership role and the membership well. He added, "I am proud to have you representing me on the board. I am also taking note to never get on your bad side."

All three variables—Head, Heart, and Action—are at our disposal if not already automatically in play when we engage in a situation, conversation, or opportunity to make a connection. I had to really work to notice my own behavior patterns to discern how I typically respond out of habit. It is with practice that I can now identify the patterns of each kind of response and purposefully adjust these responses to make even better connections with others. Let's look at each element one at a time. Remember, each has strengths and weaknesses and all three elements are tools we each can use to lead to real, lasting change in our lives and workplaces.

Head Responses

If you respond with questions or find yourself with a heightened need for additional information, you are having a *Head response*. Sometimes, you may need your questions answered before you can think about anything else. As with all three variables, there are good and bad, pros and cons; heady responses connect to a larger system and analytical detail.

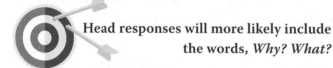

Head responses will more likely include
the words, *Why? What?*

There are both good and bad things associated with a Head response. It is our responsibility to notice not just if we are having a Head response but if there is a pattern as to when we do or do not have a Head response. It is hard for me to narrow down when I am having a Head response versus not because I am almost always having a Head response. I think there is a connection between my Head responses and when I am frustrated, excited, or taken off guard. When my brother disclosed that he made a much lower grade on an assignment than he expected, I immediately asked for the specific instructions of the assignment. He told me about the assignment, but I wanted him to read it off the syllabus. I then tried to figure out his instructor's grading rubric and why he got the grade that he did. Note that a Head response isn't necessarily an intellectual response but an analytical or detail-oriented response.

If there is a way for a Head person to be fully prepared for any given situation, they will often do it, so that when in need they can be right or, even better, righter than the next person. Head people are indispensable resources even though they aren't always that fun to be around. Once comfortable with an organization's by-laws, archived minutes, budgets, and any measured assessments or evaluations, they are free to connect, but only once this information is collected, reviewed, and mastered.

When doing party-of-one work, remember that it is both about how you respond as well as how you expect others to respond. Do you assume it's your way? This is a big assumption, but we typically assume everyone behaves and responds the same way that we do—whether or not we are conscious of our assumption or bias. A great example of a Head response paired with assumption of a Head response from another person occurred on a recent flight. The flight had boarded and we were waiting to push back from the gate and I overheard a flight attendant, let's call her Shari, sharing (loudly) with a co-worker her dismay that a passenger hadn't followed procedure. Evidently, a passenger sitting several rows behind me on the other side of the plane was causing a disruption. As I was listening to the flight attendant loudly report what was happening, I was able to pick up a few details. First, the passenger was traveling with his wife and two young toddlers. Because the plane was configured three seats, aisle, three seats, he was not sitting immediately near his family and evidently was sitting in a different row several rows away. Shari reported that the passenger kept standing up to assist his wife. The flight attendant was exasperated and exclaimed, "Why didn't he just ask someone to move before everyone got settled? That is just what you do. Duh." The co-worker looked on and didn't respond. Shari then cited particular policies and practices that passengers ought to be familiar with if they travel with children.

Here is the limitation of Shari's Head response. Perhaps this passenger isn't familiar with the policies and practices of flying with children. It is even possible that the father did in fact ask for fellow passengers to switch seats with him and was denied. These are other rational explanations—other Head response options.

Using this *Head, Heart, Action* model of understanding, I have asked participants over the years to answer one question about their Head responses or lack thereof.

What have I learned about my Head self?

"That I have expectations that shape how I act...like in school, what I expect from the teacher affects the way I present myself and do work in class. I have learned these expectations limit me from seeing my options or the bigger picture. I have learned that I really don't want to be another drone in this world, and even though I have always thought that, the depth to which I understand that has changed. I have learned that I can be "free" even in structures like school, I just have to open my mind and not set limits that aren't there. I have learned that I have in some ways become so caught up in our bureaucratic systems that I often do not listen to my inner self or feel like an individual. I need to be aware and reflective in each moment so that I may feel what I am doing. I now understand how instead of doing this I have bullshitted my own life to a certain extent. By getting done what is acceptable to the 'norm' or expectations, I sometimes do not learn or grow from my work and thoughts. I have to actively and freshly look at each task, idea, assignment, etc., to really get an appreciation of it being in my life." —M. Todd

---

Shari might be accurate about policies and practices, but sometimes it isn't a documented policy that is needed in a situation but a little empathy and understanding, even if you have to pretend. The point here isn't that the passenger wasn't following procedure, but that Shari wasn't connecting with the passenger. She stated that she didn't know what was going on and then interpreted the scenario through her own experience.

Frances Kendall, a mentor of mine and fellow social justice educator, makes a suggestion that works well for Head-responding folks seeking answers for situations that are either unknowable or unanswerable. She states in *Understanding White Privilege: Creating Pathways to Authentic Relationships Across Race*, "It's useful to keep a filter in your mind through which you run your thoughts or comments. Remarks such as *'If I were you...'* or *'I know just how you feel...'* are never very helpful in opening up communications, and they take on an air of arrogance in conversations in which there is an imbalance of privilege" (Kendall, 151). Shari doesn't actually know what is happening with this particular passenger and relies on her many years of flying experience to 1) point out that the scenario does not follow a regular pattern and 2) uses this privilege, not to help, but to arrogantly disconnect from the passenger instead of providing a space for communication and assistance.

> Using this *Head, Heart, Action* model of understanding, I have asked participants over the years to answer one question about their Head responses or lack thereof.
>
> **What have I learned about my Head self?**
>
> That I internalize the viewpoint/assumption that people who speak in slang are uneducated...and that what is unfamiliar to me may be in fact a language as legitimate as any other version of English language (American, English, British, Southern accents, etc.) and that my previous opinion was simply another example of my own racism manifesting itself and that I know nothing about anything related to the experiences of others. —D. McDonnell

As a diversity educator for the past fifteen-plus years, I turn to the many conversations about differing ideologies, lived experiences of different people, and the many ally and advocacy movements I have worked with. There often isn't a "how-to" guide for every situation, nor is every piece of relevant information readily available each and every time we need to respond to a situation or scenario. There isn't a policy for everything; in fact, writing policy is often a Head response that happens when something new occurs. It is up to us to notice when a Head response or an expectation of a Head response isn't enough. We need to adjust our responses and expectations to fit each connection opportunity. Please note that neither Shari nor her co-worker moved to assist the passengers. They both just watched the struggle until it somehow fixed itself. They didn't leap into service but stayed in inaction, an Action response. Nor did either of them show any empathy for how exhausting flying with children on a 5 a.m. flight might be or that the passenger's behaviors may be disturbing others from settling in and sleeping. They didn't have a Heart response short of ridicule.

Head responses may make sense at the time. Luckily, our Heart and/or Action elements can kick in to inform our responses at some point. Remember, all three variables exist in each of us. No amount of policies, procedures, manuals, models, vocabulary lists, and filters can prevent an error when dealing with other humans. Remember this fact as it also applies to everyone else. A Head response is often analytical but not necessarily intelligent. The need for details, options, and variables sometimes may show up in policies or protocols, but it isn't always a good, purposeful, or socially valuable response. I think of legislation that is eventually overturned or amended that at one time "made sense" and is now perceived differently. Think of the outdated practices and policies that no longer make sense with our cultural norms and community standards. For example, we used to use leeches as a common medical intervention or barred women from riding bicycles for fear of causing sterility. We followed through with these practices at the time because that is what we knew. It is always possible that better information or data will lead to changes, and in the meantime we are all doing the best we can with what we have some of the time.

There are both good and bad qualities of a Head response that depend on the appropriateness of the response and the others involved in the moment. Take this list of both pros and cons of Head-responding people. This is your strength as well as your weakness. If this isn't you, this is a good starting place to understand others who respond differently than you do to situations.

HEAD PRO/CON SHEET

Head: Why? What?

Pro	Con
• Understanding	• Heartless
• Attentive	• Too many questions
• Focus	• Resistance
• Detached (also a con)	• Paralysis/no action
• Ask hard questions	• Overconfident

PUBLIC SERVICE EMPLOYEES—
visit www.goodenoughnow.com/freebies for
worksheets, guides, and free fun stuff you can use!

NOTES

Heart Responses

A *Heart response* is a compassion-based response. Regardless of whether you are feeling for others or experiencing your own emotions—new or relived—a Heart response often connects a situation or conversation to something much larger than what is actually present. The first words that come to mind when discussing Heart ways of responding are a sense of belonging or connection to others, even those one may never meet or are not even born yet. A Heart-responding person may feel connected to ideas or communities and defend them even as an outsider. Heart responses are necessary when developing mission and vision for groups or programs and can even lead to more powerful branding conversations that are significantly bigger in scope than just the task or responsibilities at hand. They are able to personalize target membership, customers, and clients, as well as envision the future of a program long before it has been implemented so that elements can be thought of in advance way before they may even come up. Once inspired and directed, the Heart responder can make connections, referrals, and stay true to the greater mission.

Responses from this place will more likely include the word, *How?*

Just the other day, I was having a conversation with our postal service worker, Tanya, about classism, underemployment, and houselessness. As she walks our neighborhood delivering our mail, she interacts with the transient population that walks up and down the sidewalks throughout the day. Tanya knows people's names, histories, and needs and does everything she can to pay attention to these folks to see if they have eaten and are healthy, warm, and taking care of each other. The same transient population that she interacts with each and every day doesn't interact with me though I say hello and such when I am taking my garbage can to the curb.

When Tanya and I started these conversations, I quickly adjusted my response to listen to her. In our conversations I could connect the few people I would watch gather recycling out of our bins to the economic and political conversations I engage in with my friends and colleagues. My—our—community has suffered for the past few decades with the closing of the lumber mills and dairies and now even more so. Many of these folks have night shift jobs and are just trying to get by. I also learned the difference between homeless and houseless from Tanya, not just as new vocabulary words for me but as my living expectations being placed upon others who may not rent or pay a mortgage but, in fact, do make homes and build communities, just not in houses on cul-de-sacs. Tanya's Heart response consistently connects one-on-one interactions, listening to stories of suffering and need, with shared excitement and joy of real people in our community. Moreover, these individual examples seem to fuel her desire to serve the community and develop housing options and more community awareness. There are human consequences of the recent economic downturn (and the next one) that impact our own communities. "Decision makers felt the last recession because their retirement accounts dropped in value, while these folks' quality of life didn't change at all," exclaimed Tanya during one of our powerful conversations. She of course is totally right.

I have learned a lot from my conversations with Tanya. She brings up complex issues that are difficult to solve quickly. She also often shares that she appreciates my ability to just listen and hear her. Often, I believe, Tanya assumes that others just don't know the impact of these huge issues, and if she can just connect with them they will be so moved that they will have to do something. She is usually disappointed because she doesn't interpret inaction as a response. The only response that counts for her, at

Using this *Head, Heart, Action* model of understanding, I have asked participants over the years to answer one question about their Heart responses or lack thereof.

What have I learned about my Heart self?

"The one main thing that I have learned about myself throughout this semester is that nearly nothing physical or emotional can completely stop me. I believe wholeheartedly in my ability to accomplish goals regardless of what lies in my path. Another aspect of me that I came to fully realize is that I am really hard on myself, and that I use this attitude as a personal motivation. Being an intuitive thinker, I tend to view myself as a failure when I am unable to figure something out or accomplish goals at a certain standard. It gets to the point that it greatly hinders my communication with others, and even impacting my relationships with those around me. Before this semester, I never understood how much I shut myself off or stress out. It is now to the point where people have begun to notice, whereas before I was able to maintain a happy-go-lucky exterior." —T. Jones

"I've begun to kind of understand how my mind works in certain situations. Like before if something or someone got me mad I would one way or another blame myself. Ha! That doesn't happen anymore. I only take blame when I know it's my fault. I've also learned how different I am in different situations and places—and how different I am with certain people. Like, and I know I talk about home a lot, but I think that LA defines me. The people there have a different feel to me. I'm a completely different person. I feel like my responsibilities and priorities change. I'm the kind of person who enjoys alone time but feels so much happier with family around. One role that I take very seriously and think that it's my most important one is being an older sister. I'm lacking that here a little. I guess that what I'm saying is that family is me. They are important to me, and how I am now and how I will be later is greatly influenced by them and my perspective of them." —Y. Melendez times, is someone else's Heart response. Not everyone is going to respond this way. Tanya could miss an opportunity to connect with someone else because of this expectation she places on others.

In 2000, Shelia Heen, Bruce Patton, and Douglas Stone published *Difficult Conversations,* and they give great advice to Heart responders like Tanya. In order for less-Heart people to connect with your feelings, they suggest, "Don't vent. Describe feelings carefully...frame [your] feelings back into the problem [so that you can] express the full spectrum of your feelings" (Heen, 102–108). This way a connection can be made that includes your feelings and the larger impact of your response without shutting down the other person in the conversation. Even worse, a missed connection could lead to a different kind of responder being entirely disconnected from the issues at hand, leading to no further connection opportunities.

By evaluating others and your own way of showing up, a Heart person can hear and acknowledge what is being shared freely and receive the needed acknowledgement from others. A Heart response is often compassionate, but not necessarily emotional in nature. The need for greater impact or understanding of larger community groups and other aspects outside of the immediate scope of the conversation can lead to very powerful and often-times overwhelming responses, but it can often seem off topic, derailing, and overwhelming as it can be greater than the scope of the conversation. I think scenarios that seem baffling or contradictory are those that get so overwhelming that I am uncertain that any progress can ever be made.

Heart responses make sense. They may not be measureable or immediately action oriented, but they bring up difficult topics that need to be taken into consideration even if just to thoroughly examine possibilities and what is currently known. Remember, all three variables exist in each of us. We roll the dice, and we habitually respond. By doing party-of-one work, we can notice these behavior patterns and keep the ones we like and adjust the ones we don't. By learning to respond in ways that lead to better connections, we can allow others to respond their way and fill in the gaps. The pros and cons of Heart responses are important to take note of so that we can better understand others as well as our own responses. This self-reflection work leads to better connections, and that matters.

HEART PRO/CON SHEET

 **Heart: How?**

Pro	Con
• Being open	• "Calm down" backfire
• Authenticity	• Not being taken seriously
• Empathetic	• Too involved
• Listening— gather other perspectives	• Too close
• Being an ally to others	• Struggle getting the feeling to action
• Passion	• Thinking about it too long
• Awareness	• Fear decisions may hurt others
• Synthesizer	• Having no boundaries
• Being a translator	• Reacting without information
• You are loyal	

WANNA GIVE UP?
visit www.goodenoughnow.com/freebies for
worksheets, guides, and free fun stuff you can use!

NOTES

Action Responses

Ever leap into action before you know all the details? This is an *Action response* classic move! If you are filled with a need to "do" something in response to a prompt or a sense that "nothing can be done," then you are in full-on action mode. Action responses range from petitions to paralysis.

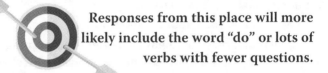

Responses from this place will more likely include the word "do" or lots of verbs with fewer questions.

I remember as a young child when I first heard that PETA, People for the Ethical Treatment of Animals, had a list of businesses to boycott that did animal testing, I sent off for a copy. My family had just come back from a deer hunting trip, and while cleaning the deer my grandmother made a joke in reference to my brother's "skinnin' skills." She said, "Boy, you better do a better job quick or PETA is gonna add you to their naughty list." I silently responded with, *"Wait!* There is a list!" The next week I rode my bike to the library and found the address and wrote a letter to request a copy of this list. I was fully committed to boycotting the businesses that were mean to animals (at the time I didn't understand what animal testing was). Weeks went by, and *finally* the list arrived in the mail. The list was long—really long. Almost everything in our pantry, fridge, and bathroom was on the list. I became overwhelmed and moved from immediate action to inaction. I couldn't do what I wanted to do. I decided then and there I would never wear fur, but I couldn't commit to anything more. To this day, I look for products that don't do animal testing and try to stay true to those brands. Thirty years later, different corporations have purchased many of my favorite brands, and I often feel like my efforts are futile, but they do matter—though small. I still don't wear fur and I, personally, am not cruel to animals. This is an Action response and party-of-one work at its best. Oddly, I still eat meat and dairy products. This is an example of incongruence between my beliefs and my behaviors.

Using this *Head, Heart, Action* model of understanding, I have asked participants over the years to answer one question about their Action responses or lack thereof.

What have I learned about my Action self?

"I have learned that I have a harder time learning about myself than I thought. I am not as good at self-reflection as I would have assumed. I don't like conflict. I avoid having to talk about difficult things or dealing with communication issues head-on. I also have learned that I can change this. I am getting better at honestly admitting things head-on. It is simpler that way. And yet communication is always hard, always messy. I give advice too much when I should just listen. I think about myself too much when talking to others. I try to make people feel important by putting a lot of effort into 'paying attention' in obvious ways. I am more comfortable in settings where I am surrounded by people of my same race and socio-economic status even though I really wish that wasn't the case. I want to figure out why and change that. I am really flexible with my identities and I adapt to situations a lot by changing my speech and behavior. Sometimes I feel like I am too good at altering my identity and don't have a solid base identity. I'm not sure who I would be if I was totally alone—without others' expectations to influence my self-perceptions. I'm pretty sure I do have a fairly solid identity underneath everything. Solid yet fluid. I do genuinely like the company of myself when I am alone. I have a lot to learn about myself as a communicator but I like learning. I have a lot of learned behaviors. I'm not sure I agree with a philosophies/moral level, but I also just find thinking about that really interesting." —K. Coughlin

Sometimes we make decisions so quickly that we don't have time to work out all of the details. I think of crisis responders as a great example of Action responders. Sure, they have had *a lot* of training and education to do what they do and care about one another on their crew and those in danger. But in the moment, they trust the training and decide quickly what to do and what not to do. I haven't had this kind of training but am quick to respond as I see things that are problematic or unsafe. My annoyed friends often chant, "Safety first!" when I lag behind because I am fixing exposed electrical cords or wrinkled carpets. I am the person who gathers shopping carts in the parking lot and puts them all away in case it gets windy. There are lots of times when I get in trouble or bother people for doing things I am not supposed to do, and I keep doing them. It is almost like I can't help myself.

This "automatic pilot" feeling can also get me into a lot of trouble. I am often too quick to respond to a frustrating e-mail, jump to conclusions, and can easily make sticky situations even more awkward. Great ideas come as quickly as bad ideas. It is the element of risk that comes into play when an Action response succeeds or fails—that is what risk is!

Even in failure, an Action person will get something from the experience that informs the next move to be bigger, bolder, and different. With clear delegation, agenda items, staff roles, and directions, the Action person can accomplish a lot by being flexible, independent, structureless, with short-term or interim positions. These are folks who are great at getting a new initiative up and off the ground. An Action-response person can sometimes be criticized for trying to "build the plane while flying it," but maybe this is better than never starting the project at all. This shows up by interrupting others yet can usually circle back to the original conversation point with ease. Whether routine or one new project after another, the work will get done, more than likely imperfectly, often better than originally planned, and will require some cleanup or retouching. When I work in teams, there seems to always be a need for someone to "clean up in my wake."

I see another great example of Action responses when looking at Congress and military interventions. (Some would say Congress is both a great example of action and inaction by virtue of being Congress!) It seems that "hawks" turn to embargos, sanctions, and military intervention and "doves" leap to mediation, reconciliation, healthcare, and humanitarian aid. Collectively, we figure out how to pay for any of these options let alone our next diplomatic move later. During a refugee crisis, is the first call to the Pentagon or the Red Cross? Former President Bill Clinton has openly stated that one of his biggest regrets during his presidency was not getting involved during the Rwandan genocide. He just didn't know what to do and did nothing. I am just speculating here, but his inaction during his presidency may now fuel his global humanitarian initiatives.

There are endless examples of uninformed action leading to misunderstanding, miscommunication, and mistakes. We have all been here. Remember, this model applies to everyone. If we all just slowed down for just a few beats of time and then acted, we might have better results. Slowing down doesn't mean never leaping, and it is very different from never ever responding at all. Responding out of reflex and a total lack of response are two ends of a spectrum with lots of options in between.

An Action response is often instant but not necessarily planned out or tested. The need for decisions, responses, and completion can build momentum and keep up with a fast-paced environment, but it can often lead to mistakes, unforeseen problems, and paralysis, inaction, apathy, and frustration.

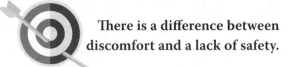

There is a difference between discomfort and a lack of safety.

It is really important to reiterate that inaction is an Action response. By doing nothing, no matter the reason, we don't act outwardly but inwardly. This is where the other variables may kick in. To keep this kind of Action response in mind, I think of bystander behavior where we often assume someone else more qualified will respond, so we do nothing. There are tons of examples, even staged news shows now on television where situations are created to see if and what anyone will do. So many scenarios, one after another, show full recognition, frustration, and the feeling of inadequacy as a witness, and the climax of the show is when someone leaps into a scenario to intervene. These altercations often take time to simmer down and the intervener with an Action response to realize the information that they witnessed was a setup. The bystanders are often questioned as well as to why they didn't intervene. These shows are all about Action responses. Both can be dangerous as well as totally socially acceptable. If you are at a restaurant and you observe another table of diners getting into a fight, do you intervene? What if you see someone volunteering to take a drunk person home? To keep this party-of-one work going, what if you have had a few drinks and someone challenges your ability to drive home? After telling a really funny joke, someone doesn't laugh and tells you that the joke is offensive, what is your response? Are there subjects that you don't talk about or words that you whisper?

In my family, everything was up for full-volume conversation, so prison sentences, cancer, affairs, politics, and hurt feelings weren't off limits. Needless to say, I didn't realize this was different until after *many* dinner parties where I brought up topics that were off limits, but I didn't know. How am I supposed to know that even though everyone at the table knows that Uncle Eddie got divorced *yet again,* this isn't conversation material? I think the word is "decorum" for knowing when and when not to do certain things as well. I am still learning this. Bystander behavior is about doing nothing when you could intervene. *To be clear, there is a difference between discomfort and a lack of safety.* We will discuss this more in Chapter 4.

Action responses may seem habitual, be based on trained muscle memory, or just seem to occur without a second of thought. There are both pros and cons to Action responses, and these can change with even the slightest variant in a situation or perspective.

ACTION PRO/CON SHEET

Action: Do/Action Verbs

Good	Bad
• Get it done	• Waste energy
• Problem solving	• Too quick to take action
• Results oriented	• Not collaborative/ more dictatorial
• Accountability	• Too honest
• Responsible	• Bossy
• Leadership	• Controlling
• Adaptable	• Manipulative
• Action with minimal data	• Not good listeners
• Independent initiative	• Prevents buy-in
• Eagerness to implement	• Narcissistic
• Intuitive	
• Charism	

HEALTH SERVICE PROFESSIONALS—
visit www.goodenoughnow.com/freebies for
worksheets, guides, and free fun stuff you can use!

NOTES

Do You See You?

I see you.

Do you see you?

Head, Heart, and Action responses have equal value. There isn't a better or worse variable, but certainly the impact of our responses is worthy of judgment. All three variables are at our disposal all of the time—just like a Magic 8-Ball. Chances are one or two of the variables you can identify with as your go-to response style. Perhaps there is one that you know you don't utilize at first. It is even possible that you respond differently in different contexts, be it at work, home, place of worship, farmer's market, or a dark parking lot after a full day of travel. Our responses vary based on our circumstances and lived experiences. These variances start by us writing stories about the present moment pulling from our past experiences, knowledge, etc. We make judgments and assumptions based on these stories to feel safe and prepared. It is what we do with them that matter. Remember, it matters to matter and our best starting place to reclaim responsibility for who and how we show up, no matter the context, is party-of-one work.

Use this space to map out your own *Head, Heart, Action* response habits. Can you identify specific examples of these elements showing up in your behaviors? What about others? Does anything change in a different context? What do you do (Action) to be prepared (Head) and safe (Heart)?

	Head	Heart	Action
You			
Others			

**YOU PICK!
HEAD, HEART, ACTION SHEET**

POLITICIANS—
visit www.goodenoughnow.com/freebies for
worksheets, guides, and free fun stuff you can use!

NOTES

CHAPTER 2

THEM

Follow me here. I just sat down after getting today's mail. As I sort through it, there are different piles that form—to recycle, to do, to pay, to read, and to respond. I decide instantly what I will do. I take action. Even if I decide to read it later, that is taking action. It is up to the sender of the mail to get me to categorize it in the manner that they want me to. Let me back up a second—today's mail included an envelope that says, "Did we do something wrong? Renewal information included." I felt a sense of panic. "Crap! What did I forget to renew?" I open the envelope and realize it is junk mail and then I put it in the recycling bin (Action). They got my attention by pulling on my internal calendar (Head) and maybe a little on my heartstrings for making me feel guilty (Heart). Guilt, or compassion, is the biggest motivator for mailings that include pictures of children or animals, just like the pieces with statistics or discount codes motivate the analytical sense of reason. Expiration dates connect with a reader's sense of Action. Junk mail, to be successful, has to tap into all three—Head, Heart, and Action—or it never gets our attention. This is the same way we may adjust how we present an idea or request to someone else so that it gets their attention.

> When reading an early draft of this book, Loren told me he didn't know about the red envelopes. I guess you would only know this if you have ever been *very late* paying bills.
> A few days later, one of our dogs got sick and he raced to the cabinet and remarked that the spot remover was in a red bottle for emergencies.

If you can grasp the marketing strategies of junk mail, the leap to working with others shouldn't be too much of a jump. When your electric bill arrives in a white envelope there is a different outcome than if it arrives in a pink one and completely different if it arrives in a red envelope. I have experienced embarrassment and an increased sense of urgency based on an envelope color just like when I am listening to someone speaking to me with various tones of voice, language choices, etc. When I see red envelopes, especially if they are letter size and not card size on someone's desk, I still have a reaction and it isn't even my mail. Similarly, I can overhear a conversation and I can write a story about those conversing based on their tone, sound level, topic, language use, and the receiver's level of engagement.

If the electric company keeps stock of different color envelopes to elicit different responses, we can also do this.

If we respond differently to different sizes, colors, shapes, and thicknesses of envelopes, we can take notice.

There is meaning here that matters.

If the electric company has a red logo and the marketing department designed only red envelopes to be congruent with the brand this might make sense in a Head-Action way, but not necessarily in a Heart way. Yes, a customer's favorite color might be red and they love the envelope, but because of other business practices it is more likely that customers would have a negative reaction to a red envelope because other businesses reserve these envelopes for bad news. This matters to both the company and the customer—the sender and the receiver.

Another new strategy I have noticed in my junk pile is handwritten fonts. The materials are mass printed but look like they are handwritten. Even subscription card services are available to look like handwriting. Nothing beats a real handwritten note, even in my terrible, illegible handwriting—it is the time, effort, and thought that counts.

What is imperative to notice is that all three elements are needed to accomplish any given task in the best manner possible, be it customer service, thank-you presents, or diplomacy. All three elements can be purposefully harnessed in our daily responses as well as how we roll out different programs and initiatives or engage in conversations.

A well-meaning and thoughtful Heart response I recently experienced was in the shape of a Harry and David holiday fruit basket. I was given this expensive gift as a token of the sender's appreciation for me and my work. The box came to my home while I was out of the country so I asked my partner to open the box, knowing it might be perishable. My partner, Loren, is an environmental ethicist and was overwhelmed by the amount of packaging material, most of which was not recyclable, and the thoughtfulness of the gift was lost. My partner is a Head-Heart person, so the action of giving a gift and me receiving a gift was overwhelmed by the grand impact the item itself has on the planet—therefore, an irrational gift to give. For the record, the pears were outstanding.

To truly connect, matter, and communicate effectively with one another we need to be mindful of all three elements in us and in others. This isn't profoundly new, but this concept has yet to really take hold in our self-awareness, personal development, and communication habits.

So what? I often ask myself this as well when I have learned of yet another personality assessment tool or quiz. I question the validity unless I like the results; then I see it as valid. This is because I am a Head person and I follow almost everything up with questions. Questioning authority, facts, situations, etc., is something I learned as a child that I seem to turn to even more.

Questions from a Head person are often "Why?" "When?" "What?"—detail-oriented questions. They can be imperative to a situation as well as distractions and can seem irrelevant. I think of the scene from *Stand by Me*—after one of the shyer characters tells an amazing story about a pie eating contest gone wrong, one of the other boys asks, "What did you have to pay to enter the contest?" These details can solve mysteries and lead to eye rolls for missing the point.

I would imagine more Heart people may question, "How do Head, Heart, Action responses impact others in a positive and/ or negative way? I don't want to offend anyone. How can I be the best person and make as few mistakes or negative impacts as possible? How come (insert person here) doesn't understand me or another person better if this is so simple?" This unanswerable line of questioning can result in a "So what?" response as well.

For my fellow Action people, let's be honest—I'm lucky if you are still reading along and haven't been distracted by something else by now. I did include charts and tables for the quick skimmer in you! Action people may want to know what to *do* with this information. "What is the quickest way to master this and get others to do it too? How can this simple paradigm shift be implemented on the largest scale?" asks a Heart-Action person. "Where does this need to start happening first to be the most effective for change?" asks the Head-Action person, "I don't get it—I need more!" may be the response of the Head-Heart person.

Use this space again to map out your own Head, Heart, Action response habits. Can you identify specific examples of these elements showing up in your behaviors? What about others? Does anything change in a different context? What do you do (Action) to be prepared (Head) and safe (Heart)?

PRO/CON BLANK SHEET			
	Head	**Heart**	**Action**
Pro			
Cons			

STUDENTS—
visit www.goodenoughnow.com/freebies for
worksheets, guides, and free fun stuff you can use!

NOTES

Can you identify any behavior patterns of yours (or others) that are at least two of the variables? What are some pros and cons of these kinds of responses?

PRO/CON COMBO SHEET

	Head	Heart	Action
Head	Head/Head	Head/Heart	Head/Action
Heart	Heart/Head	Heart/Heart	Heart/Action
Action	Action/Head	Action/Heart	Action/Action

SALES TEAMS—
visit www.goodenoughnow.com/freebies for
worksheets, guides, and free fun stuff you can use!

NOTES

The problem is that your "them" isn't absolute. Someone in the "them" group sees you as their "them." Real change doesn't lie outside of us.

Go back and circle all of the examples that are about someone else and their behavior patterns. If you are stuck, reflect on those close to you—friends, family, co-workers, neighbors, etc.

Pointing fingers. That guy! You don't know this one woman I work with—it is always her fault. If it isn't one other person's fault, it is a group of people outside of ourselves. *Them!*

Perhaps it is easier for us to focus outside of ourselves to develop the tools and/or habits to look inward. This is by far the most common refrain I hear after more than fifteen years of diversity trainings and social justice education work. It is always something outside of us—outside of our control or our responsibility. This is why nothing changes, or if things do change it's for the worse.

Change can happen in a number of ways—socially through our relationships, communications, teamwork, personal engagement; financially through increased sales, accumulation of more loyal clients; or even culturally through racism, classism, homophobia—we all have many options for change we are charged with focusing on in our work and in our personal lives.

When you add up all of the "us" groups and "me" groups out there, you are left with "we."

The problem is that your "them" isn't absolute. Someone in the "them" group sees you as their "them." Real change doesn't lie outside of us. This is why all of the work you have already done likely hasn't been revolutionary or even evolutionary. Real change is in the "us" and the "me" groups. When you add up all of the "us" groups and "me" groups out there, you are left with "we."

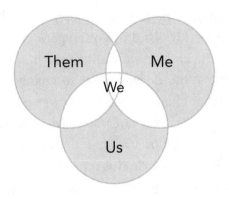

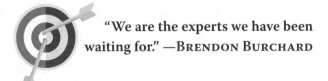

"We are the ones we have been waiting for." —HOPI PROPHECY

In the following pages, I present to you an anecdote for misplaced optimism that will cost you—financially, emotionally, or otherwise—next to nothing. I am not a dream crusher nor a pessimist. Where the ideal and big dreams collide with realism, scarce resources, hiring freezes, and quickly accelerating expectations of exceptionality—this is the concept of Good Enough Now.

Think of Good Enough Now like a rephrasing of "in the meantime." While we are waiting around for the answers, what do we do in the meantime? We need to be introspective and take responsibility for who and how we are in the world.

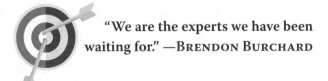

"We are the experts we have been waiting for." —BRENDON BURCHARD

I hear you. I am a hot mess too. I have an irrational fear of ladders, and ten minutes ago I thought my television was broken because I was using the wrong remote control. What if, in the meantime, I am in fact the best tool I have to be the change that I want to see in the world? Gandhi is often paraphrased when we talk about "becoming the change we want to see in the world." There is something to this. What do you want to change? What have you done today to be that change? Want a cleaner planet? Did you pick up a piece of litter? Did you not purchase something with excess packaging? Did you walk or use shared transportation options to run that errand? Even if you do this once, you are being the change.

If we can collectively do the best we can with what we have some of the time, I believe deeply that radical change will occur in our individual and collective lives. Sitting around pointing fingers and waiting for change to appear on the horizon hasn't worked thus far to my satisfaction.

What if, together, we shift our own paradigm and play to our strengths, support others in their strengths, build better teams, serve others better, and create spaces were people want to be and want to stay?

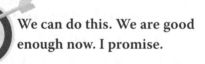 We can do this. We are good enough now. I promise.

While on the presidential campaign trail, Hillary Clinton was having a brief meeting with two men from the #BlackLivesMatter collective. The two men talked about excessive violence and brutality and its impact on the greater community. I would say they were Heart and Action oriented in their delivery. Hillary Clinton responded in a Head-Action manner stating, "We can't change hearts. We can only change policy." This made it through the media cycles as a communication blunder and misstep on

Clinton's part. What I think got missed is that both parties were coming from a common Action space. One side was more Heart and the other more Head, but Action was in common. They were differently on the same page. Being different while on the same page can open up a space for more conversation.

What is imperative is to develop the habit of noticing how we each show up in conversation. Once we begin to notice others and ourselves, we can meet up in a common way and, with trust and respect, listen to a different perspective. The vulnerability and strength to recognize that a different perspective is needed to improve your own is a radical paradigm shift. I need difference so that my strengths and their strengths can do the best.

Referencing his own "2006 Aspiring Social Justice Ally Identity Development Conceptual Model," Keith Edwards cautions Head-oriented people regarding "[the] over-intellectualization in which an individual may be paralyzed to inaction by fear of making mistakes and not being the 'ideal ally.'" This is reason enough to read this model without committing to it 100 percent. Moreover, you don't want to not engage at all out of fear of failure—just try to keep trying. In a model on how to be an ally, the model itself can steer you wrong. Please don't overthink or overly rely on this model as *the* answer on how to fix *them* or to justify why you are right. This is a framework for your own self-reflection and better connections with others.

To keep a kind of Heart response in mind, I think of the Founding Fathers and their words in the Declaration of Independence, where "all men are created equal." The largest scope imaginable energizes this ideal of a new country full of opportunity, to those who are seen as human. The sense of compassion wasn't yet attributed to any women, indigenous people, slaves, and/or people of color, not to mention children, those without a formal education, illiterate folks, the poor, the disabled, those with mental illness, etc. Equality was (and is) limited to certain humans, but this gets lost in the details of a broad vision. This model, too, will have limitations and is in need of further study largely due to my own limitations, habits, and comfort zones. My bias, lived experience, access to a diverse community of resources, and identities are limited. I developed and will share this model anyway and hope for edits, further research, and the start of a conversation.

Action folks, I know you don't believe me—so let's look at three people. If you don't believe me after this or your paradigm doesn't shift a little, then there is a much bigger problem than this book can address. Remember, you are one of the archetypes and you should be able to name folks in your life who are the other two.

Let's take that guy. You know the one. He has totally "drunk the Kool-Aid." Everyone loves him except he is a pain to work with. Somehow others forget how difficult he is and the difficulty is overlooked time and time again by co-workers, management, and the general public. He seems infallible even though you know, as do others, of lots of mistakes and questionable decisions he has made. This guy has a clear vision bigger than menial tasks and details. He has people who are loyal and devoted, so they manage the details. He is the face of the particular project, mission, or team. He probably has addiction issues, acts impulsively, and leaps to conclusions without the full context. However, every once in a while he connects with a particular system or informational source and he is unstoppable. If you could only figure out how to capture his laser-beam focus on the one thing and the charisma that he carries effortlessly with him, you could really get something done.

X _____

Or what about that woman over there? You can't get her to act. Asking her where you should go to lunch becomes this epic conversation or some sort of *Consumer Reports*-level research begins. You just want lunch. Stories about memories or personal experiences mixed with Yelp review data, directions, distances, and details fill your lunch hour. You might conclude, "Forget it, I will just pack a lunch tomorrow." It is also awe inspiring, perhaps after you have eaten, how much information and connection she has from a simple question. She is a collector of every angle, perspective, and historical experience for the variables in question. This much context may leave her at times doubtful, feeling apathetic or indifferent to outcomes, and most importantly overwhelmed by the significance of everything. What pulls her out of what may appear like dramatic navel-gazing is a simple awareness of something that can be done. Once a choice is made to act, she is on fire and unstoppable. How do you help her not deviate from this one task or be distracted from the flood of research that could occur and the ever-present unanswerable questions? Moreover, how can you harness the creativity, connections, and contemplation that would lead to significantly better decisions and action plans?

X _____

Then there is the often-cold, strictly business person. They don't spend a lot of time looking at your vacation pictures or dreaming up big collaborative initiatives. They have the facts, evidence, data, or information needed and explicit directions to move forward and accomplish the task at hand. Don't get me wrong, they can be a great person, flexible to work with, caring and compassionate, and fun to be around, but these aren't the first impression elements that stand out. This person will be late to their funeral to get that one more thing done. While on family vacation, they may stop by and visit with clients while in the neighborhood. Their style is efficient, but doesn't always land well on others.

Interestingly, while they may not realize that they come off heartless, they are often a sensitive person. They don't always know to think about others unless it is on a to-do list. You could help by telling them to loosen their tie and take off their jacket while responding to a crisis to look more approachable. They would do it, but might not think of this on their own. They follow directions well. Every once in a while, some connection will be made, often between two unrelated elements, and they will ignite a passion that others, and even they, didn't know was in there. Once they care about something, they will figure out a way to analytically succeed. Wouldn't it be great to be able to somewhat magically place the necessary yet seemingly unrelated collection of facts near enough to each other that this person could stumble into them and develop working solutions? This makes me think of the movie *The Princess Bride,* when a wheelbarrow and a flame-retardant cloak save the day.

X _____

What is important to note when reviewing these three characters is that each of them has strengths and weaknesses. They are right and wrong. They are exactly what you need and frustrating to work with. All three of these types of people are different, and differently right. It is up to us to figure out how to work with them so that we can all benefit. For us all to be good enough now, we have to see in others their strengths. To do this, we have to first identify our own strengths and weaknesses. If we can place ourselves into a model and notice our own behavior and response patterns, this habit can be transferred to others.

Let's name the first example, Leo. Leo is all Heart and Action. The second example, let's call her Zoey. Zoey is Head and Heart oriented. Last, the third example, let's call Sky. Sky is Head and Action. For the record, these names are my three dogs' names. This model works for all groups. Have you figured out which one you are?

Leo is my cuddle bunny social dog. He is an active dog that prefers to be with me or lots of people. He knows he is so ugly he is cute. In dog training school he was the best student, I think because he knew that got him more attention and treats. We would come home and he would do whatever he wanted and largely got away with it. Leo is the only dog that sleeps in our bed.

Zoey is known as Princess Anxiety-Pants. She is often indecisive and terrified that we will not return from a trip, outside of the house, or the laundry room. She is by far the smartest dog in that she can lift a wok off the stove and eat its contents silently, but she then feels terribly guilty and mopes around the house afterward. She is very vocal, often with indecision or anxiety, and very loyal.

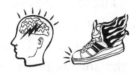

Sky is a Catahuola, a trained ranch dog, and her breed is known for hunting wild boars in the forest. She is quick to learn new tricks and is best at "stay" no matter how long or what temptations we put in front of her. Her laser-beam focus is at times terrifying and as noticeable as her speed when chasing something. She got fired from the ranch because she was gun-shy, and the loud noises hurt her sensibilities.

All three are great dogs. All three are different in different ways. As our dogs' people, we have learned or been trained by them to treat them as they wish to be treated. Tony Alessandra's Platinum Rule®[3] is as much at play here as it is with our relationships at home and at work. Alessandra extends the Platinum Rule to customers, team members, co-workers, and the like. We already do this with pets really well. I believe we can do this better with people.

The concept of the Platinum Rule is to treat people as they wish to be treated, unlike the Golden Rule, which is to treat others how I wish to be treated. How I wish to be treated may or may not be similar to how someone else wants to be treated. To find out how someone else wants to be treated, I believe you have to listen and notice how they show up. Moreover, I believe we need to start with others being differently right. Not everyone is *my* way. Even someone who is similar to my way isn't always in every way

---

3   For more information about the Platinum Rule, e-mail AJA@Alessandra.com.

my way. If I can notice how they are different, I can also notice how those differences are strengths, perhaps in a different situation. All of our differences will make better teams. A team of too many similarities is how nothing actually gets done or improves through creative innovation and experimental risk taking.

Even the three characterizations earlier—though they are very different from one another, frustrating and mystifying—I see in myself all three.

The three characters above—who did you think of? Go ahead and write that down here. (Remember, you are one of them!)

_____

_____

_____

_____

_____

_____

_____

_____

_____

_____

_____

_____

_____

_____

_____

_____

_____

_____

_____

NAME SOMEONE SHEET

	#1 Kool-Aid	#2 Yelp + Memories	#3 Robot
	Leo	Zoey	Sky
Go-To Elements	Heart + Action	Head + Heart	Head + Action
Third-Rail Element	Head	Action	Heart
You?			
Name Someone			
Name Someone			
Name Someone			
Strengths			
Weaknesses			
What do you notice about this person?			

MEDIATORS—
visit www.goodenoughnow.com/freebies for
worksheets, guides, and free fun stuff you can use!

NOTES

Please note that the folks you named, the archetypes from earlier, and our own behavioral patterns combine two of the three elements almost all of the time. Each of the individual elements has both positive and negative characteristics as seen in the earlier pro/con charts on pages 54 (Head), 61 (Heart), and 69 (Action).

These participants self-identify which group they want to work with and are tasked with making up a collective list. Typically, the Head group writes a list and then makes me a shorter list of the highlights or the most popular responses from the group. The Heart group makes sure everyone can see and hear the conversation and ensure that all voices are heard equally. This group usually hugs after they are done. The Action group usually finishes first, doesn't follow directions to the letter, and is loud and rowdy.

Remember, our differences are right in different contexts. Our strengths can come in handy and can deter progress. Our weaknesses can hold us back and can limit mistakes, risk, and errors. We are differently right. Through coming at situations differently, we can be differently right and do the best we can with what we have most of the time.

Head, Heart, and Action elements are ways of describing how we habitually show up in the world and in our relationships. Two of these elements are our "go-to" places, while the third is our power element. The power in this third place is what prevents us from responding in certain ways. It actually provides us with the realistic motivation to get out of our own way and nurture our dreams and visions and overcome our personal struggles during hard times and scarce resources.

Head, Heart, and Action as behavioral patterns aren't new concepts when reviewing self-help books as well as business growth books. However, pairing these behavioral patterns with a sense of responsibility and self-reflection completes the Good Enough Now model. Pulling from the *Courageous Conversations*

Compass: "Emotional (Feeling) responses are seated in the Heart, intellectual (Thinking) in the mind, moral (Believing) in the soul, and social (Doing) in the hands and feet" (Singleton, 20). Here, the "solution" to facilitating challenging conversations with courage, the participants have to first identify the source of courage. This parallels nicely with Head (thinking), Heart (feeling + believing), and Action (believing + doing).

The sourcing of our sense of courage typically comes from many of these elements, and this is both what makes a conversation challenging as well as imperative to have in the first place. Typically, our patterns of responses stem from two of the three variables. The third or remaining variable is still a part of the way we show up in the world and in our relationships. As mentioned earlier, this third element I often refer to as the third rail, like in the New York City subway systems. There are the two rails that the train runs on, and the third that is electrified. Two rails do the work. The third rail has all of the power. Chances are that a really challenging situation or conversation that garners an unusual response from you trips your third rail and that is why it may need more courage to confront. It isn't a habit...yet. Doing "party-of-one" work is about taking note of your usual response patterns as well as uncovering the unusual, out-of-the-ordinary challenges that have come up in your past so that you can use all of you and your history, or lived experience, to make better and more authentic connections with others.

The three archetypes from earlier, Kool-Aid, Yelp, and Robot, are real people. I have chosen these three people as the archetypes of a Heart-Action, Head-Heart, and Head-Action person because they exemplify how we can all do different right. Like them, we too have our shortcomings, and like them we will be remembered for the lasting impact we leave behind in our personal and professional legacies.

Though he struggled with alcoholism and self-identified as a womanizer, Dr. Martin Luther King Jr. accomplished a lot with his dream and outsourced to others a plan. He showed up and served as the face of a movement and still does to a certain extent because of his dedicated Heart- and Action-oriented motivations. He wrote about his lack of certainty and his self-serving agenda for equality for white, Christian, straight men and black, Christian, straight men. It is when King's work embraced a tactical economical system (Head) of working toward a living wage that his work led to real lasting change in which he found a sense of confidence.

The year 2016 closed with Mother Teresa being sainted. For most, this seemed inevitable, but it is her pattern of questioning her beliefs that had prevented sainthood. Her Head and Heart "go-to" habits led her to feeling apathetic and doubtful that any action, big or small, would make any kind of difference at all. Of course, we would all agree that her work mattered, despite the lack of resolution to work against hunger and suffering, but this is because we collectively know that this is an issue larger than one food pantry or a simple program could solve. Yet her work mattered. She found motivation in her actions, her third-rail power element, even though her head and heart continued to question everything she believed in. Mother Teresa started by building a school, and that mattered.

Last, the third example is credited for coming up with the concept of non-violent civil disobedience and informed both Martin Luther King Jr.'s and Mother Teresa's work. Gandhi, though Head and Action oriented, was terrible at school. He didn't care about the system of education and felt isolated from it as a first-generation college student and a subpar law student. After being fired time and time again for seemingly not caring about his clients or his cases, Gandhi traveled to South Africa where he found his voice and his passion. As he wrote in his autobiography, *The Story of My Experiments with Truth*, the tactic of non-violent disobedience came out of his noticing that when he wasn't beating his wife and children, they responded better. No one generally thinks of Gandhi as a violent person, and yet it was a rational conclusion drawn from two unrelated experiences that altered how he protested British rule. He was methodical in his actions until he realized that he could impact hundreds of thousands of people around the world (Heart). As Gandhi connected to his heart, he fought to benefit people he might never meet. He found a sense of compassion in truth and became unstoppable.

I think we can all agree that Martin Luther King Jr., Mother Teresa, and Gandhi fought a good fight. Each had self-limiting beliefs or personal disconnects that had to be overcome to do the right thing. They each did the right thing differently. We can too. Once you are aware of who and how you show up in your life, you can seek out complementary yet different counterparts, colleagues, and support networks. Who knows, the answer may be in the next cubicle from you.

By working with each other's strengths and our different ways of being right, we can work with what we already have to do something differently. We can be good enough now.

The patterns that run our life, the third-rail power element, are where our shortcomings, excuses, and personal kryptonite live. Interestingly, the third-rail power element is also where our self-motivation, determination, and resilience come from.

Martin Luther King Jr. attested that his work got far more effective when he switched from focusing on his own agenda and development and expanded his view to a living wage for all. As a Heart-Action person, he often didn't know if the work he was a part of would make a systematic change. When he linked his vision with an economic goal of fair payment for fair labor for all workers, he used his third power element, Head, and gas pedaled his own way through his own excuses, and his work became more threatening to systems of oppression. He knew that this was the right work to be doing and that it might cost him his life. After receiving the Nobel Peace Prize, King spoke for a second time in October of 1964 at Oberlin College, giving a speech he called "The Future of Integration." Looking forward to the upcoming presidential election and just after President John F. Kennedy's assassination followed by riots in six (or more) cities across the United States, murders of civil rights workers in Mississippi adding to an already violent year, King stated, "The time is always right to do what's right.... It is true that behavior cannot be legislated, and legislation cannot make you love me, but legislation can restrain you from lynching me, and I think that is kind of important."[4]

Mother Teresa, too, found her effectiveness exponentially increased when she took her calling, Head-Heart, and connected her observations and experiences to possible actions of serving others. As a young child she felt her calling to her faith. After being trained in Dublin, she took her vows in 1931 and for almost two decades, until 1948, Mother Teresa worked as a teacher in Calcutta, India, at St. Mary's High School. These seventeen years of witnessing the extreme suffering, pain, hunger, and poverty of her local community lead to her doubt and apathy. By questioning her faith, she became even more faithful. Her self-awareness and self-reflection grew her sense of calling, but led to little action that she deemed worthy of serving others. In 1948, Mother Teresa's superiors granted permission for her to leave the convent school and serve in the hardest, most impoverished areas of Calcutta. This became her turning point. Mother Teresa stayed true to her faith, head, and heart and paved the way to serving slum children by building a school. She had no funds, volunteers, or other forms of support, just her consistent dependence on her divine Providence. This work is the foundation for what became Mother Teresa's own order in 1950 called "The Missionaries of Charity" with the focus "to love and care for those persons nobody was prepared to look after."[5]

4   "The Reverend Dr. Martin Luther King Jr. at Oberlin," Oberlin.edu, accessed November 08, 2016, http://www.oberlin.edu/external/EOG/BlackHistoryMonth/MLK/MLKmainpage.html.

5   Evon Elias, "The Angel of Mercy – Mother Teresa of Calcutta," Chaldean.org, September 6, 2007, http://www.chaldean.org/CommunityPages/ChaldeanChurches/MartMariamIllUSA/tabid/136/articleType/ArticleView/articleId/175/The-Angel-of-Mercy-Mother-Teresa-of-Calcutta.aspx.

Gandhi also had a major revelation that significantly changed his work. As a Head- and Action-oriented person, it was his Heart work that led him to the concept of civility. In his autobiography, *The Story of My Experiments with Truth,* Gandhi stated, "Civility does not here mean the mere outward gentleness of speech cultivated for the occasion, but an inborn gentleness and desire to do the opponent good" (Gandhi, 437). As Gandhi developed his focus on nonviolent civil disobedience, he leaned on the ideal of satyagraha, or truth. The Metta Center for Nonviolence defines satyagraha and Gandhi's focus like this:

> A satyagrahi is a person who is dedicated to truth (*sat,* or *satya*), or more specifically one who offers satyagraha or participates in a satyagraha campaign.

The requirements Gandhi laid down for his satyagrahis include:

- Having a firm commitment to nonviolence, simplicity, honesty, chastity, and self-discipline in thought, word, and deed.

- Holding firmly to the truth (Sanskrit *a-graha*), that all life is interconnected.

- Rejecting violence in any form, including humiliation of opponents, accepting humiliation of oneself, or the violence toward oneself implied in the use of intoxicating substances.

- Forgoing material comforts for the greater good of all beings.

- Relying always on soul-force when it is necessary to resist another's behavior.

Satyagrahis trust that the opponent can be awakened to compassion, and cultivate an unwavering faith in the goodness of humanity, constantly separating person from deed.[6]

Making Better Connections

I hear you. There are times when I too am intimidated by my heroes. There are other times when I just want to watch television for hours and eat food I regret later. I get it. Remember, your heroes and my heroes feel/felt the same way. We don't have time to wait for someone else to solve the problems that we can identify. The self-reflection necessary to take responsibility for our own habitual behaviors doesn't have to be a self-deprecating exercise. Claim or reclaim responsibility for yourself—the good, bad, ugly, and awesome. Figure out the patterns in your own life and where they came from, then determine which you want to keep and where you need to make some edits. Believing we are good (at least at something) is imperative. Once we can know where our strengths are, we can lean into these areas and recruit others to support us where we need the most assistance. We can also do this for others. The key is to remember that we are all doing the best we can with what we have some of the time because we are enough. Even "that guy" is enough for something—enough to somebody. If we approached and engaged one another as well as introduced new initiatives, policies, and plans with these concepts in mind, we would make better connections. This is super simple, but not so easy to do regularly. To do this, and for real change to occur, we have to do something different.

---

6   "Satyagrahi - Metta Center," Metta Center for Nonviolence, accessed November 08, 2016, http://mettacenter.org/definitions/gloss-concepts/satyagrahi/.

FRANCHISE OWNERS—
visit www.goodenoughnow.com/freebies for
worksheets, guides, and free fun stuff you can use!

NOTES

SECTION TWO

ENOUGH

Good but different. Once we have a firm understanding of *who* and *how* we are in the world, we can then do something different. We all come with strengths and weaknesses, habits and comfort zones, as well as limitations, biases, and inexperience. Please note that I don't mean 100 percent different (usually) but a focused different that keeps the parts you like and challenges growth in other areas. This is what it means to be enough to get started.

It is with self-reflection and noticing others' behaviors and responses that we can decide what of ourself to keep, challenge, and/or change. To best connect, matter, and communicate with others, it is up to us to value our patterns and those of others. We have done our "party-of-one" work and look at *"them"* to highlight what is already good.

Perhaps our good is in line with what we think or feel it should be and maybe not. Perhaps we have a lot of self-work to do before we can improve our connection and communication with others. The key here is to believe that we are enough.

Enough doesn't mean perfect, but the base of what is needed to proceed. There will be improvements made, unavoidable mistakes, and better versions out there. In the meantime, let's do the best we can with what we have some of the time. That is more than enough.

The goal of development is to foster a more complex and sophisticated consciousness that is more stable and less likely to regress or recycle through earlier statuses (Kegan, 1994). As a result of these constant changes in the individual and the environments, the ally for social justice status is an aspirational identity one must continuously work toward (Edwards, 53). Meaning our work is never done. As soon as you feel competent, you have to start all over and repeat the process to uncover more areas of work.

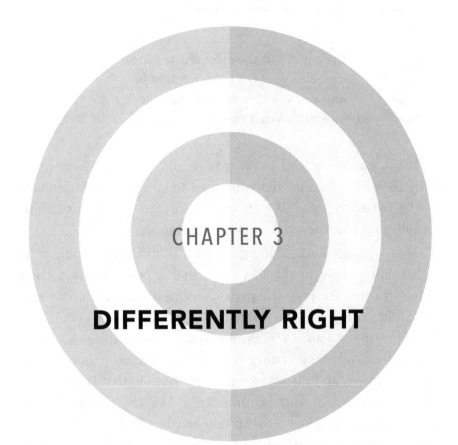

CHAPTER 3

DIFFERENTLY RIGHT

Thirty seconds. What if you can provide a thirty-second window to others to see what they have to offer? What if you could do this for yourself? This is what I mean by differently right. I am not slipping down a relativistic slippery slide here; I mean to consciously allow for others (and yourself) to have a small space to occur in a way other than what you expect.

When you realized I was talking about Martin Luther King Jr., Mother Teresa, and Gandhi, chances are there were elements you didn't expect. This doesn't make you terribly wrong, you just didn't know. You may look at them a little differently, but that doesn't take away the impact they had on our world. Can you apply this tiny window of space to the *"them"* players in your life?

If you pick out the most frustrating person in your life (which might be you) can you give enough space for complications that you didn't expect?

If you can get to this point, you might be able to hear something they have to offer that you need to connect, communicate, and be better together. We all are the way we are because of our complicated histories and ways of being in the world.

First with my heroes, King, Mother Teresa, and Gandhi, then with other people in my life, I reached a point where I could stop and listen for how the person in question got the way they did. Doing this became a habit until I found myself giving even me some space—not excuses, but space—for getting this far in my own journey. My history is standing here with me just like theirs is. If we can fully stand with one another, that is more than enough to connect and communicate. We are responsible for who and how we show up with one another. We are responsible for doing our own work on what it took for us to show up in the first place.

Once you know where you stand, you can see the turning points. The turning points may be something you wish to forget or perhaps something you wish to repeat. Either way, they are fundamental in how your Head-, Heart-, and Action-oriented behavior patterns develop. Typically, the turning points, or crucible moments as I like to call them, of your life will come from your third-rail power element. This is a pattern that I notice as to why these moments may happen to or even with someone else and impact the individuals differently. This is how the same experience can have dramatically different impacts on others. Some may be changed for life while others don't even notice the event.

Moreover, we can experience the same event and have different impacts, results, perspectives, etc.

For example, our parents raised my brother and me until I was nineteen, and he was almost sixteen. Our mother passed away while I was away in college, and my brother was at home with her. He, as a Head-Heart person, was impacted by the death of our mother differently than I was as a Head-Action person. As adults now, twenty-plus years later, this crucible moment in our lives manifests differently. He is much stricter about going to the doctor for examinations and much more likely to obsess (his word) about illnesses, bruises, moles, etc., turning into cancer. I am more likely to carefully pick the people I get close to and make quick judgments about others or keep my distance long after I need to. He has an Action-based response of going to the doctor, working out, and doing everything he can to prevent illness, aging, and death. I have a Heart response connected to personal loss and lack of control of others' outcomes. Same experience—differently right responses from our third places.

After you figure out what your "go-to" response is, you may also determine what your number-two response is. It is responses from your number-three place that are your crucible moments in life. These experiences will forever alter your character and how you behave or respond in the future.

It is possible that someone hasn't had a crucible moment or struggles to pinpoint one from many. This piece of the conversation of self-awareness isn't to promote how terrible or perfect one's life has been. Crucible moments can be life-changing moments that are overwhelmingly positive. Divorce, death, graduation, success, failure, disappointment, surprise, shame, fear, joy, pride, and many other experiences, actions, inactions, thoughts, and feelings can lead to moments that forever stretch, change, and grow one's self-actualization.

Remembering that all three elements—Head, Heart, and Action—exist in all of us, use this space to identify your own go-to response sources (your number-one and/or number-two element). It may be easier to identify the element you go to the least, often dismiss, etc. The third-rail element is always with us and fuels our excuses and motivates us during crucible moments. There also isn't a value difference between the number-one and the number-two response pattern source. All three elements are equally as important and ever present.

	#1	#2	Third Rail
MLK	Heart	Action	Head
Mother Teresa	Head	Heart	Action
Gandhi	Head	Action	Heart
You?			

I wrote several reflection guides, called *Notice Notes,*[7] that I use as training tools to help participants notice how they respond to a given scenario. There is one example I often use as a demonstration of a crucible moment in my own life. I tend to react most commonly from a Head or Action place—this is just one experience where I responded (or didn't respond) from a Heart place and I am a different person because of it.

A large man gets on a Southwest flight. As he is getting to his seat, the flight attendant checks her sheet and loudly announces this passenger has only purchased one seat. She further challenges the other passengers to watch and make sure his seatbelt fastens. The passenger, crying and humiliated, sits down and buckles his seatbelt. The other passengers and the flight attendant immediately look away as if nothing happened, leaving the man in tears.

This was an incredibly powerful experience for me as it was from my number-three place. I had an emotional reaction rooted in my own body image issues and struggles with my own weight. I sat there and did *nothing*—and I am an Action-oriented person! Luckily, my friend, the large man, still talks to me and it was with his help that I was able to uncover these emotions. This is a *great* example for me of how a reaction from your number-three place is a life changer.

If you now take a second to reflect back on your life, what are the turning points (positive and negative) that got you to where you are today? This isn't a competition, just a place to reflect on your own journey. This journey may be made up of many crucible moments or just a few. For some, doing this kind of self-reflection exercise may be the first time you have ever done anything like this and perhaps, over time, this will become a crucible moment.

---

7   *Notice Notes* can be found in my store at www.goodenoughnow.com.

Key Crucible Moments in My Life	+/–	My Third-Rail Response (Heart Responses for Me)
Losing State Championships	–	Public failure
Death of my mother	–	Loss of control, hurt, entitlement
Experiencing the sunrise in Kenya	+	Awe, noisy silence of the jungle, the world is so much bigger than me
Advocating for a young rape survivor	+	Came to terms with my own survival, injustice, unfairness, real bias exists
Striking out on my own	+	Independence, freedom, fear of the unknown
Being medically evacuated from the Peace Corps	–	Dependency, inability, determination, stubborn, pain, loss, no closure
Opening my first after-school program in South Carolina	+	Determination, community, doing good, joy, the power of group laughter
Being the most conservative person on staff in Oregon	+	Shock, feeling of home, Texas pride, odd duck, importance of listening without judgment
Coming out	+	Pride, scarcity, power, fear, danger, acceptance, love, intimacy
Learning about privilege	+	Denial, ignorance, injustice, whiteness, questioning authority, real trust, shame, guilt
Leaving an abusive relationship	+	Loneliness, fierce power, fear, confidence, self-doubt, manipulation

Key Crucible Moments in My Life	+/–	My Third-Rail Response (Heart Responses for Me)
Getting sober	+	Determination, addiction, self-worth, health, mental illness, anxiety, depression
Putting my cat, Bob, down	–	Closure, death, celebration, deep sadness, family, friendship, need for connection
Meeting Loren	+	Comfort, no performance, inspiration, joy, adventure, safety, stability, worthy
Starting my own business	+	Terrified, fulfillment, creative, fear, fraud, confidence, powerful, vulnerable, generous, curious, authentic

There are a ton of experiences that made me who I am, both good and bad. Most crucible moments have positive and negative lessons and impacts. This is just a sample of my crucible moments. As a Head-Action person, I notice that the act of making a list of crucible moments is somewhat habitual for me. Naming the Heart-related, third-rail responses was way more challenging than I expected, and this is my model!

These experiences show up in the present day even though they happened in the past. When the popular and beautiful Erica Huntington[8] from my sixth grade reading class asked me to go to the Bruce Springsteen concert with her, I didn't know that this would be relevant in my adult life thirty years later. I live in fear of being tricked and have a very high "need to know" element that shows up in my work, friendships, and casual encounters with strangers. Somewhere in me is the little girl who was left at the Dallas Convention Center after the concert. Erica had been dared to take me to the concert. I didn't know this and everyone

---

8   Name has been changed because I honestly don't remember.

in class the next day did. I didn't know that me walking into class with my concert T-shirt was the punch line of the joke. Unknowingly, I vowed that this would never happen again. Perhaps this is where me being the center of attention, storyteller, and jokester started?

As a starting place, self-reflection often starts by looking backward at major turning points in one's life. Perhaps you ask why something happened or wonder in the moment why something is occurring, but it isn't until sometime in the future that we make reason out of the experience. The lesson of the experience, though, remains in the act or life event itself that then informs the reasoning that may occur later. The reasoning may inform our feelings or behaviors in the future, but these life events are critical in how we teach ourselves to show up.

In many instances, life has happened, and I have then worked to make meaning of what has occurred. I have learned in what Warren Bennis and Robert Thomas in "Crucibles of Leadership" call "crucibles"—"transformative experience[s] through which an individual comes to a new or an altered sense of identity. Some of these crucibles were searingly painful...[o]thers were unanticipated learning opportunities that present themselves whether I wanted them or not.... Still others, I sought, and, while they were definitely uncomfortable, felt essential to my understanding" (Kendall, 3).

This act of looking back is about reviewing your own lived experience and looking for the valuable learnings so that you can see yourself and others as differently right. It is our lived experience that is our most powerful connection tool.

> I [Ariana Huffington] am convinced of two fundamental truths about human beings. The first is that we all have within us a centered place of wisdom, harmony, and strength. This is a truth that all the world's

philosophies and religions—whether Christianity, Islam, Judaism, or Buddhism—acknowledge in one form or another: "The kingdom of God is within you." Or as Archimedes said, "Give me a place to stand, and I will move the world."

The second truth is that we're all going to veer away from the place again and again and again. That's the nature of life. In fact, we may be off course more often than we are on course.

The question is how quickly can we get back to the centered place of wisdom, harmony, and strength. It's in this sacred place that life is transformed from struggle to grace, and we are suddenly filled with trust, whatever our obstacles, challenges, or disappointments. As Steve Jobs said in his now legendary commencement address at Stanford, "You can't connect the dots looking forward; you can only connect them looking backwards. So you have to trust that the dots will somehow connect in your future. You have to trust in something—your gut, destiny, life, karma, whatever. This approach has never let me down, and it has made all the difference in my life (*Thrive*, 8-9).

Give it a whirl.

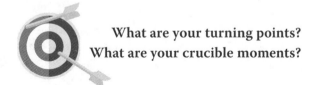

**What are your turning points?
What are your crucible moments?**

CRUCIBLE RECORDING SHEET
Fill in the blank

I am _____ (name)		**I see myself as a** (check one) ☐ Head ☐ Heart ☐ Action **person.**
Key Crucible Moments in My Life	**+/-**	**My Third-Rail Response** Write down the appropriate category (Head, Heart, or Action) below.

COUNSELORS—
visit www.goodenoughnow.com/freebies for
worksheets, guides, and free fun stuff you can use!

NOTES

Our personal growth isn't anyone else's responsibility but our own. This starts with the belief that we are enough.

As you review all of the crucible moments in your life, you will find deep wells of experience that serve as resources for others. Your strengths are fueled by these moments in your life. Our behavioral patterns follow through from all of our lived experiences. Once we are more familiar with our own treasure chests of lessons learned, we can listen to others sharing their own. Being vulnerable with one another creates an environment where we can all feel safe and prepared. This sense of belonging is more effective than any management training system and requires no additional funding. Allowing space for someone to really connect with another takes time and is the true treasure that leads to better fellowship, productivity, and connection. Understanding each other and our own authentic self empowers each team member to ask for assistance and serve one another through our strengths. It is through this service that we can be generous with our experiences and provide each other with a genuine sense of curiosity to leave room for edits, learn, and grow with each other. It is in these spaces where loyalty, commitment, and responsibility bloom.

It can be very difficult to lead others through a self-discovery process of naming even one crucible moment. Sometimes, this is due to a young age or lack of lived experience, and other times the difficulty lies within a simple lack of awareness or acknowledgment of one's self—being unaware of how one is in the world.

> If you take [stories from past movements and faith] seriously it isn't about trying to minimize the difficult moments in your life, the painful aspects, but about engaging them, making them sources of strength-making a priority out of our relationships, our compassion, and using our intelligence and skill to challenge what's destructive (Glen Gersmehl, friend of P.R. Loeb, *Soul of a Citizen*, 307).

Here are some examples of crucible moments from a recent training I did. Perhaps these people's lived experiences will help you to listen for new information about the person sharing or even uncover your own crucible experiences.

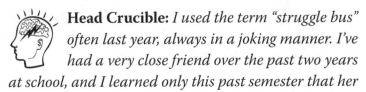 **Head Crucible:** *For me, the moment happened in high school. During my class trip, there was an incident involving shoplifting. There were three upper-class white girls whose parents worked at the school, and they stole merchandise from Chinatown. When it was discovered that someone had shoplifted goods and the items were found in the purses of the three girls, they blamed another classmate (in the same group as them) who was not as high class and was Latina. When we got back to school, everyone was interviewed first about the Latina student. The three girls made up a story about how she snuck the items into their bags. The student being accused was a friend of mine, but because I wasn't there I couldn't argue for her side and felt helpless. She was told the consequence if she was guilty was two-week suspension, being kicked off the team, and not walking at graduation. The three girls were found guilty after a two-week process, but were suspended for two days, didn't miss any varsity games, and walked at graduation.*

Head Crucible: *I used the term "struggle bus" often last year, always in a joking manner. I've had a very close friend over the past two years at school, and I learned only this past semester that her*

youngest sister has Down syndrome. This really puts into perspective the way things you might say could be affecting the people you hold closest to you without ever knowing.

Head Crucible: *I believe my crucible moment was coming out to my parents as a [gay man]. It was the first time in eighteen years of my life where I stood my ground on who I was and wasn't going to let others tell me what I am. I felt more in tune with myself and felt that I had control of what was happening in my life. Coming out empowered me to take more chances and love myself for who I am. It was through standing my ground that I was less likely to take [crap] from my brother and figure out what I want to do with my life—realizing that I am an individual who can forge my own path in life.*

Action Crucible: *I failed my nursing practical exam. I, in that moment, felt utterly like a failure. I went to my debate house after that and cried at the podium. I saw my life being miserable. I was doing something I hated and wanted to run away. I yelled at my mother after that because she pushed me to stay with it when I knew what I should be doing for myself. I told myself that day I was done and I did something about it eventually, although it took more time.*

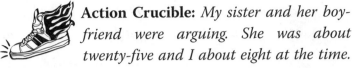 **Action Crucible:** *My sister and her boy-friend were arguing. She was about twenty-five and I about eight at the time. They always argued so this was no big deal. Then he raised his hand to hit her and I remember jumping up from watching TV and just started punching him in the stomach.*

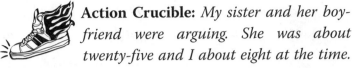 **Action Crucible:** *One day I was talking to my mom and we were reviewing each other's day thus far. She seemed flustered and began to explain that a "black man almost hit my car today!" I was shocked when she said this and asked not if she was okay, but rather why she chose to specify the color of his skin. She blankly stared at me and shrugged. I asked her if the man was white would she have said that, and without hesitation she said "no." This made us think for a bit, and I've honestly never noticed any racist or negative/similar comments from her since then. I'm rarely action oriented so I felt that this was a good time for me to stand up and actually say something.*

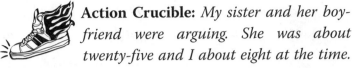 **Action Crucible:** *I was at my aunt and uncle's house last summer and I was talking to my cousin whom I had not seen in a long time. He was telling me about how one of the windows on his car had been smashed in, and he was sure it was someone from the Section 8 housing down the hill, where "all of the black people" live. It was disheartening to hear such a thing come from him, as the rest of my family is very open and welcoming. I just sat and awkwardly listened, and I still wish I had called him out.*

Action Crucible: *The first time I saw someone digging through the trash to find food. She was in her mid-twenties, a white woman wearing a nice skirt, but it showed me that hunger can happen to anyone. It was painful to watch for me, and I wanted to help her by giving her some money, but I froze because I began to overthink her agenda and wondered if I was intruding on someone else's business.*

Heart Crucible: *A crucible moment in my life was probably becoming an orientation leader. This is the first time I actually had real and authentic conversations with the voices in my head. I also began to truly embrace my identity while also being cognizant of how my identities and privileges influence the way that I show up in groups and in life in general. I continue to learn more about myself and the people around me and try my best to meet others where they are.*

Heart Crucible: *When I was in high school, we had a Day of Silence for LGBTQA people and I coincidentally had to take a make-up math test in a room I wasn't used to with teachers I wasn't used to. One of the teachers was wearing a rainbow cloth ribbon thing that had been handed out for the Day of Silence program. Another teacher came in and said to her, "Geez! Why don't you just make a whole outfit out of that stuff?" She then rolled her eyes* *and left the room. I was really upset (I wasn't out yet and I was looking for people to trust). I realized that adults could be just as mean (or meaner) than high-schoolers.*

Heart Crucible: *One day I noticed a ramshackle fort/tent in between two garbage bins. I had noticed it often as it was near a grocery store in my town. Further checking proved it to be a homeless man with all of his possessions who was attempting to live there. I was filled with a lot of emotion, I'm not really sure why, because I didn't know him or his backstory. But for some reason I just wanted to give him something, like money or food. A few weeks later, the fort was gone. How many others do I not notice?*

Heart Crucible: *My most recent crucible moment was during a party when one of my friends got too drunk and was being "persuaded" by a guy to go home with him. She had never slept with anyone before, and as a friend I didn't feel that she was in an appropriate state to make that decision. I became more emotional about the situation than I ever expected, definitely different than how I would normally react.*

Ally Development

At first glance, the term "rising sophomore" may have led you to write a story about a college freshman you know, you as a freshman, maybe even your own children. What would happen if we shared with each other crucible moments to build better connections, share with one another, and really listen for a person's lived experience instead of just coming at a conversation as an obstacle to overcome?

If listening to one another as if we would prepare to be an ally for each other happened regularly in our personal and professional lives, imagine how things might show up differently. Keith Edwards's model of *Identity Development of Aspiring Social Justice Allies* parallels this process nicely.

First, we often show up as an *Ally for Self-Interest*, which is primarily motivated to protect those that we care about from being hurt. We focus on our inner circle of people and self without thinking of those outside of our realm of influence. Moreover, folks in our inner circles are often accepted for their good intentions without considering the ways they may perpetuate the system of oppression. We do not quickly dismiss or demean those closest to us as potential allies.

This model also takes into consideration that it is often hard and unrewarding to work for those outside of our inner circle. Altruistic behaviors may make us feel good in the short term, but we often don't keep up this work. Perhaps shame or guilt prevents the continuation, or even more likely as soon as we start with one issue we uncover a hundred more and get overwhelmed. If not overwhelmed, we can also experience burnout just like Mother Teresa. We can lash out, be difficult to collaborate with, and even be defensive like Martin Luther King Jr. We can also distance ourself from other members of our own group(s), strategically defining ourself as an outsider or different like Gandhi. Head folks like Gandhi may see the system intellectually, but focus on other members of the group as the real perpetrators. By vilifying other members of our own group, aspiring allies distance themselves from others in an attempt to minimize the guilt stemming from their increasing awareness of unearned privilege afforded to those in our own group (Edwards, 47–51). This is where I may feel like a "good one" while being able to identify others as the "bad ones." It took me years to realize I was in fact an alcoholic largely because I could look at other alcoholics and see that I had a job, partner, etc., and they didn't; therefore, I wasn't like them. Moreover, I believed for a long time that I couldn't be racist because I wasn't a member of the Ku Klux Klan (KKK)—they were the racists. In order to get different results, we are going to have to do something radically different. We have to find ourselves in each problem and address these concerns one at a time as habitual behaviors on our own part.

Freire explains that rationalizing "guilt through paternalistic treatment of the oppressed, all the while holding them first in a position of dependence, will not do" (49). In this way, *Aspiring Allies for Altruism* fail to recognize that one *"must speak with the oppressed without speaking for the oppressed"* (Reason, et al. 1). To really do this, I have to take responsibility for who and how I show up and really listen to others. By speaking with others, I can gain more and more clarity that will lead to better connections with others.

Again, this isn't a step-by-step how-to manual about how to make lasting change or to be more self-aware. I would like to think that we are each more complicated than a dresser from Ikea. This process is also not linear. Much like directions on a shampoo bottle, there are just a few steps, but you repeat often. You also need to clock out and take breaks. Doing what you can with what you have some of the time is the goal. If you have identified your strengths, it is through acknowledgement of your weaknesses that you learn where to grow and develop. I now realize that I am both an alcoholic and have been sober for more than a decade. I also now know that racism isn't just reserved for KKK members and shows up in different ways, many of which I must be mindful of, acknowledge, work around, and do better. It is through listening and connecting with others that I can monitor my addictive patterns and my own racism. I decided to quit drinking and pay attention to my own biases while holding the incongruence of eating meat and not wearing fur.

If you need a step-by-step process, I encourage you to take note, actually notice, how you show up (and don't) in your own life. Noticing your behavioral patterns is the first step. Once you notice the patterns, try to avoid making meaning of them or justifying the behaviors; just take notice. Take note of the response patterns that you like. Keep these. Take note of the response patterns you don't like. If you need to, check in with someone who knows you really well to find out if these unfavorable patterns really do show up. If so, and you still don't like it, now you have a place to start focusing on for your own personal development. You may also uncover some patterns that seem incongruent. These are important as well. You might want to keep them, change them, highlight them, or work toward these behaviors more closely aligning with what you in fact do value. This is a simple process, just not easy work...and remember to take a break. Come back to the work when you need to and you are ready to do the work again.

The concept of enough is that there isn't an end to the process, nor can one accomplish enough and be done. There is always more work to do, undo, and redo. As Hazel Wolf says in Paul Loeb's *Soul of a Citizen*, "You hike, run a river, or watch birds in a park. With all the things to observe, there's less room for worry. Your mind gets a rest. You come back ready to take on Exxon" (Loeb, 314). Otherwise, you will be dealing with burnout and that is never good. Burnout is how good work stops cold in its tracks. We cannot carry the burden of everyone and everything all of the time. This leads to compassionate exhaustion, as compared to radical amazement, where one cares so much they lose track of themselves and can no longer show up for themselves, let alone others. Often, for some, showing up at all is an act of revolution. Getting out of bed, assuming they have one, to show up at work or even the dinner table, to be seen and to interact with others can be such a struggle that asking them to grow or be uncomfortable isn't possible. We need to develop a sense larger than ourselves while (re)claiming responsibility for ourselves.

By fostering a motivation to be an ally that is less dependent on the perceptions of peers, student affairs professionals could develop more consistent social justice allies. I wouldn't limit this to just student affairs professionals, but as individuals interacting with one another both in and outside of work.

> The progression from *dependence* to *independence* to *interdependence* has been observed in Goodman's (2000) Continuum of Self-Interest as well as other identity development theories (Edwards, 42-43).

Knowing *who* and *how* we show up is an ongoing process that allows us to try. The act of trying depends on a conscious act of connection with ourself and with others, knowing that perfection isn't the goal. For any change to occur, we must do something radically different than just expecting the same things to render new outcomes. Waiting around for others to do the heavy lifting doesn't seem to be working. I believe that the onus lies with each of us to take responsibility for our own lived experiences and how these crucible moments both impair and motivate our desire to connect and communicate with each other. This is the radical difference needed to consciously foster truly innovative, thriving, and inclusive communities of all of our lived experiences, good, bad, ugly, and awesome.

> Without the communion which engenders true cooperation...the [oppressed] people would have been mere objects of the revolutionary activity...and as objects, their adherence would have been impossible. At the most, there might have been "adhesion," but that is a component of domination, not revolution. In dialogical theory, at no stage can revolutionary action forgo

communion with the people. Communion in turn elic-
its cooperation, which brings leaders and people to...
fusion.... This fusion can exist only if revolutionary
action is really human, empathetic, loving, communica-
tive, and humble, in order to be liberating (Freire, 154).

From the pamphlet "If talking is so important, why is it so
hard?" by the National Hospice and Palliative Care Organization:

[There are] many opportunities and ways to raise the
issue [of difficult topics]. Once you realize how many
"conversation [starters]" there are in daily life, you will
be ready to start your own conversation. And starting
is the most important part. Too often, these conversations don't take place until there is no time left for
honest discussion, reflection, and planning.[9]

Honestly, what cost do you have for some of the conversations
you aren't having? I say some, because in some instances there is
a life-or-death, safety-based cost that I don't want to undervalue.
However, most of the conversations we avoid stem from work that
we need to do on and with ourselves. Going back to our lived
experiences as a tool, the best tool in fact that we have at our
disposal—moments of achievement and failure—is still informing
how we show up now. Believing that with all of these struggles
we are actually good enough now is critical to shift the paradigm.
Once we can see others as differently right, perhaps we can leave
room for ourselves to grow and evolve and learn.

The first stage of almost any identity development or change
model is *ignorance*. This doesn't reference one's intelligence, but
the lack of exposure or knowledge of something new. It isn't until

---

9   National Hospice and Palliative Care Organization, "If talking Is so important,
why is it so hard?" National Hospice and Palliative Care Organization, page 1, accessed
November 9, 2016, http://www.caringinfo.org/files/public/brochures/Conversations
_booklet.pdf.

we come into contact with something new that we can learn from it. For the vast majority of us, how we habitually show up (or don't) is often news to us. Those close to us may have knowledge about us and our habits that we don't know about. Think about your friend who got fired, again. She may be completely dismayed as to why she would get fired again. Do you know why she is difficult to employ? Manage? Work with? Of course you do—you like her anyway. You know them better then they know themselves. Before you go giving yourself a blue ribbon, be mindful that your close friends do this to you too. They know things about you that you can't see.

Let's go to the last time you were *defensive*. If you can't think of a time, ask someone close to you. They might tell you the truth. If they don't, you can take notice for a week and see if you can determine when you are responding on the defense. Even better, determine if you respond defensively from a Head, Heart, or Action-oriented response place.

Typically, I respond defensively out of guilt or shame, which is disguised as a lack of control. Brené Brown[10] has done a lot of research on vulnerability, and in her book *Daring Greatly* my biggest takeaway was that I fear being vulnerable because I have connected a lack of control with weakness. I am certain this is left over from the crucible moments connected to my mother's sudden and, to me, unexpected death. A response pattern for me has been to tightly control as many variables as possible so that I will never be surprised again. Spoiler alert—I have still been surprised by the unexpected speeding tickets, gate changes that led to missed flights, as well as being scooped up from the airport and

---

10   Berry Liberman, "Brené Brown Is a Grounded Researcher," Dumbo Feather, 2012, http://www.dumbofeather.com/conversation/brene-brown-is-a-grounded -researcher/#sthash.l7jdC6bf.7P6E1zMN.dpuf.

taken out to a romantic dinner or stumbling into my own surprise party. Vulnerability isn't about weakness but the strength to be open to both the good and the bad of living a full life. Paired with curiosity and generosity, I am a better listener with few expectations being brought into a conversation. It takes strength to believe in myself enough and trust that I am as prepared as I need to be. I must believe that I do not need to depend on my tools, resources, and contacts to deal with life's twists and turns; I can depend on myself. If I bring my personal strength to each interaction, I have less need to be right and more room for the unknown that leads to better connections with others in the moment. If I connect better and more authentically with others, I have less of a need to be right, decreased interest in proving them wrong, and can be more consistently conscious of my intentions and the impact for which I am responsible. I have less need to be on the defense and can just be.

 If this isn't where you want to start—try *procrastination.* Pay attention for a week and see if you can identify what, when, and how you procrastinate. Again, no judgment here, just taking note of a habitual behavioral pattern. Procrastination tends to occur because we lack the time, means, energy, and/or passion. We fail to act because we talk our way out of it, feel inadequately prepared, or just don't want to. Perhaps you procrastinate making a decision because you are seeking more information to make the best decision possible. There may not even be a strategy or plan in place so inaction is the only good choice, and we put off the decision of doing nothing because we are uncertain of how to even do nothing.

 Don't worry, there are more—what about *deflection* (sometimes disguised as delegation)? Distancing one's self from a group is a common way to deflect and not engage in something. We often think that being different or creating space between others results in a "them" and a "me." Individually, I can't be held responsible for what "they" do. I hear this a lot about the "ugly American" overseas. The "ugly American" is loud, bold, rude, self-absorbed, selfish, crude, and doesn't take the time to really understand others. Reality check—I don't have to leave the country for these things to be true about me given the right circumstances. We can also deflect by passing the buck, kicking the can down the road, or assigning responsibility to someone else. "Voting doesn't matter." "Voting in Texas doesn't matter." "They will never turn out to vote, so my vote doesn't matter." "I voted, but it doesn't matter, because who knows what the Electoral College will do anyway." "Yeah, my candidate won, but who knows how they will actually be in office." Deflection may change the subject or delegate responsibility to a different problem at hand or even to a larger system that is out of our control.

Can You Try?

So what would happen if you did something different? If right now you had all of the tools required to be enough and be differently right, what would you confront? What could you change? Who would benefit from your reaching out to them? What would happen if you tried? Who would you connect with if you tried?

CALL CENTER MANAGERS—
visit www.goodenoughnow.com/freebies for
worksheets, guides, and free fun stuff you can use!

NOTES

CHAPTER 4

LEAVING ROOM FOR EDITS

You need nothing outside of yourself to do the best you can some of the time. I have zero expectation that you commit to self-reflection, powerful connections, and authentic conversations 100 percent of the time with every single person you come in contact with. Zero expectation. What if with one person during one conversation once a day, even one day a week, you try to do something different? You can do that!

Where this gets challenging for me is to practice this for myself. Perhaps it is the extrovert part of my personality, but I find talking out loud with others easier than my inner dialogue. I needed to practice noticing behavior patterns and the Head, Heart, Action model with others before I could look inward. It wasn't until this became a habit that I could really begin to practice with my inner voice. Both need to occur. This is the ultimate chicken and egg conversation. I don't care which one fits best for you to try first, just do it some of the time until it becomes a little more comfortable and then raise the bar and start again.

As you begin to notice your two "go-to" response patterns, dig up the roots of these behaviors, decide what to keep and what to change, I want to assure you that you have the tools needed to excel. Remember, Head, Heart, and Action elements exist in all of us. Two of these elements are typical and comfortable. The third element fuels our excuses and self-limiting beliefs as well as motivates us through our crucible moments in life. This fuel is what I like to call a "gas pedal," and it is exactly what you already have at your disposal to try some of the time.

> As you notice response and behavioral patterns in others and in yourself, it is important to not make meaning of these patterns and just notice them for what they are.

Remember that these patterns often exist as a result of a crucible moment that we have lived through and inform our responses consciously or unconsciously. We are responsible for the roots of our patterns and need to leave a space for others to be differently right. We are all more complicated than we project to others. Providing a sense of space is key to better connections and communications.

> We present a story about ourselves to others.

This story is how we consciously express ourselves to others and how we want to be received, identified, validated, and perceived by others. It is also true that we may unconsciously present a story that is in alignment or incongruent with how we believe we present ourselves to others. Either way, others write a story about us. We cannot do anything about their story about us. Over time, they may alter this narrative, but that is up to them. This makes sense and may leave you saying, "Yeah, it is their work that needs to be done." The bad news is that you can't make them do anything. The good news is we can get to work on the stories we write about them. We are responsible for these stories and we can edit them accordingly.

> To truly feel unsafe, one needs to feel danger or harm. To be uncomfortable is different—where growth and risk occur without a likely result of violence or harm.

Often in diversity trainings we are told to never ever make judgments and assumptions about others. Then we do. When we get caught or even catch ourselves, we might get defensive, come up with reasons for them, or even do nothing but freeze in our tracks—caught. Instead of feeling like a failure, why don't we just work with the stories we write? Instead of trying to never do something we do all the time, let's just work with the stories we write and leave room for edits.

We write stories about others for two really good reasons. First, we need to feel safe. Second, we need to feel prepared. There is no value judgment here for either of these reasons. The key, though, is that we might not be right. Now, I am not saying that we are wrong—no, no, no—just that we might be able to be, well...righter.

What if we take these stories that we write and just reference them as drafts instead of final products? By first noticing the stories we write about others (and ourself) we can print these stories out. Now we know what we are working with and we can look at the stories as flexible components based on choices and habits. Part of being enough is anticipating edits, changes, and new aspects; fixing bugs; addressing errors; and leaving room for improvements. If we print our draft stories out triple-spaced with extra-wide margins, we are looking for feedback, suggestions, comments, and edits. Leaving room for edits isn't possible without writing a draft in the first place. It is the expectation of change that allows the draft to be edited. Our lived experiences inform the draft and our in-the-moment connections with others lead to edits that make us...righter.

Again, some will need to start with outer rather than inner work; others will be the opposite. Either way, all of the work needs to be done and redone. Start where you like and take note of the stories that we write and practice anticipating edits. Listen for more accurate and/or new information and update your stories accordingly. More often than not, instead of making edits in our stories, we rewrite new information to fit our story instead of changing the narrative. We are more likely to write a very complicated story than just make an edit. If we listen and receive new or more accurate information from the very source we are writing about, it would make sense that we just make changes so that we are righter, but instead we believe we are already the rightest we can be; therefore, they are wrong to hand you edits. If we adjust and listen with curiosity, we will expect new information. We then aren't wrong, but are editors.

I have a friend whom I never wanted to have meals with because I would get embarrassed at her long, detailed, and particular way of ordering anything off of any menu. She always needed extra this, none of this, this on the side, and would often ask questions that would bring the chef out to explain the pans used, types of oils, and base ingredients for items of interest. I wrote a story in my mind about her being a particular kind of control freak. I then saw everything she did with this "control freak" story in my mind and found myself being less and less interested in pursuing a friendship with her.

One day in particular, she started asking questions to other participants in a workshop. I felt myself backing away and getting embarrassed, when I noticed that she was turning red with hives and was struggling to breathe. Soon she couldn't ask questions anymore and ran out into the hall. I recalled her many conversations with chefs about nut derivatives and noticed someone in the meeting room eating shelled peanuts 100 feet away. I turned to the hall and dialed 911 at the same time. As I shut the door to the room I asked someone to get help immediately as my friend was having a severe allergy reaction and listened to her for direction. In that moment, I was the only person she trusted as she reached for her EpiPen. I quickly read the directions and twisted it open for her to administer as medical professionals arrived. I wasn't wrong; she is particular, and I edited my story about her, which was limited, to include a life-threatening set of allergies that need to be taken seriously.

> Just because it isn't a problem for you, doesn't mean it isn't a problem. I didn't know until this moment the privilege I have of no serious allergies.

It is important to note that, of course, we can also be utterly and totally wrong. Our stories can be completely false, inaccurate, and nowhere close to the truth. This is a real truth that we need to also take responsibility for and repeat time and time again. Our own conscious and unconscious positive and negative bias may lead us to habitually write a story that isn't based on fact. This makes me think about 2008 presidential nominee Senator

John McCain of Arizona when an audience member questioned him about the then democratic nominee, Barack Obama, being a Muslim. First, there is nothing wrong with being a Muslim. Second, now-former President Obama doesn't identify as a Muslim. McCain listened to the woman and simply corrected the inaccuracy of the questioner's story.

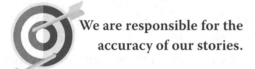 We are responsible for the accuracy of our stories.

To go one step further I would say we are 100 percent responsible for our connection with another. We often shy away from these kinds of connections because we don't feel like we are enough to play a role in the communication. If not us, then who? We must try. The idea of trying and trying sooner than later is the best way to make a change. Waiting for the exact answer, precise tools, and perfect solution hasn't really worked for us thus far. Perhaps believing that we are enough will be just different enough to result in something new.

Briefly mentioned earlier, the concept of Bystander Behavior—first penned by Alan Berkowitz and introduced to me by Mike Dilbeck and the Response Ability Project—talks about the importance of intervening. In order to act, we must have a firm understanding of how we act, when we act, and when we don't. Paralysis is an action- or inaction-based response as well. To interrupt a situation you must take several aspects into perspective. Based on your own history, is this a moment when you feel safe and prepared to not be a bystander? If not, then reacting in person may not be best. Perhaps making a phone call, bearing witness, using your video camera, or something of the like can help the situation while also keeping you feeling safe. Please note there is a significant difference between discomfort and lack of safety.

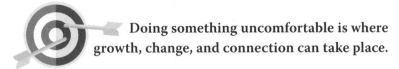 **Doing something uncomfortable is where growth, change, and connection can take place.**

Any situation, whether you act or not, can inform future situations. Being mindful of this for the next time counts. Being mindful of the patterns of a given situation also matters. Taking responsibility for similar situations that do in fact involve you is even better. Interestingly, if you do act by intervening, delegating someone else to do something, or something similar, others are far more likely to act as well. Others may be inspired to intervene next time, change their own behaviors, or take notice and claim responsibility in the next similar situation.

In a training for trainers program, Stop the Hate! Fighting Bias and Hate Crimes on Campus, we learned that acts of violence might be directed at individuals, institutions, or entire communities. Community violence has a direct impact on individuals, and violence directed at individuals also affects the community. Any act of intervention can lead to real lived experiences changing for the individuals involved and potentially on an even larger scale. Bias, both positive and negative, can lead to prejudices, which can develop into hatred and acts of violence. These acts don't have to be criminal to be powerful. Just like our acts of trying don't have to be lethal to be effective. If we were to take known war crimes from history (or present day for that matter) for example, what would have happened if someone had intervened early on before ideas grew into movements that affected millions of people? Interestingly, intervening with others is often easier than intervening in our own behavioral patterns, but these patterns can be just as powerful.

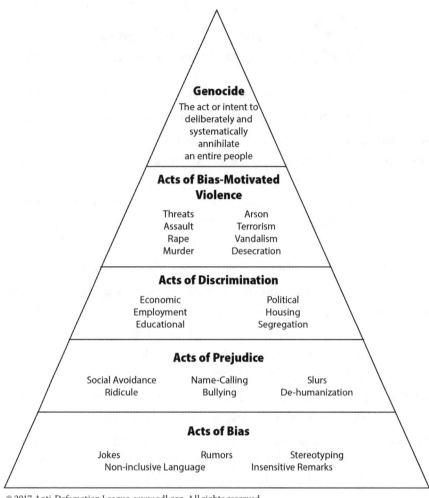

Genocide
The act or intent to deliberately and systematically annihilate an entire people

Acts of Bias-Motivated Violence

Threats	Arson
Assault	Terrorism
Rape	Vandalism
Murder	Desecration

Acts of Discrimination

Economic	Political
Employment	Housing
Educational	Segregation

Acts of Prejudice

Social Avoidance	Name-Calling	Slurs
Ridicule	Bullying	De-humanization

Acts of Bias

Jokes	Rumors	Stereotyping
Non-inclusive Language		Insensitive Remarks

If intervention could happen earlier, it is possible that larger problems could be addressed. Often, we react to an incident instead of a larger issue and then, incident after incident, time passes and the issue grows to something devastating. If, for example, we take the issue of patriotism, positive bias would be applied to those communities that have a more patriotic story written about them, like those serving in the military, serving in political office, even residents who fly a U.S. flag at their front doors. The inverse is the negative story about those that do not enlist or dodged the draft, don't vote, embezzle tax dollars, or burn a U.S. flag. It is up to us to take notice of the stories we write concerning the issue of patriotism and the patterns of our behavior in response to positive or negative incidents. How do our feelings about patriotism change during war? During the Olympics? During an election? We are responsible for these patterns in our own responses or lack thereof. We are also responsible for others' stories. This is true connection and community.

 **Raising a fist of awareness, marching in the streets, striking a picket line, kneeling on the sidelines, and staying seated are all responses that matter.**

If we feel safe enough to intervene, we can do so with a sense of generosity that allows the other person's lived experience to exist while editing our own story. The key is to believe that by being enough, we can connect and possibly intervene before something bigger, more devastating, disconnecting, and violent occurs. We can be the change we are looking for if and only if we know who and how we show up and provide space for someone else to show up differently right. From this space, we can leave room for edits to our own story and intervene at the incident level. Moreover, when someone challenges us, we can pause and listen instead of responding out of defense, deflection, or by freezing. We can show up with the strength of vulnerability to authentically connect with the person intervening with us and edit our own story. We can try. We can grow.

The book *Social Excellence: We Dare You* defines *social excellence* like this:

Social Excellence {n}: A state of perpetual generosity, curiosity, positivity, and openness to limitless possibility; a desire to intentionally connect with others; the ability to engage in deep, meaningful conversation; acting in a responsible and respectable manner, with high expectations of others; being authentic and living every day with integrity as the best version of yourself; being confident and vulnerable; being fun and compassionate; being open, kind, and bold; the deepest level of societal participation and contribution (Mattson, 21).

Genuine *curiosity* means wanting to learn more (Ibid., 87). Being kind is at the root of all *generosity* (Ibid., 93). *Authenticity* is when you and others recognize and connect (Ibid., 100). Sharing personal stories and being trustworthy with those shared with you during and long after these connections and real conversations ignites the strength of *vulnerability* (Ibid., 110). In order to grow, we have to take that first step. Each iPhone gets released hoping that all of the bugs have been worked out, and each is prepared for the unknown. They release the phone anyway. A Facebook friend of mine has been hired by Apple to hack into the new products to test for weaknesses, bugs, and errors. Apple is preparing for mistakes as best they can, yet they know that nothing will ever be perfect. Even if a product was released in a state of perfection, technology and user needs are ever changing. Advocating for change works the same way. The belief is enough. Enough is the ability to try.

Robert Nash has done extensive research that carries over to this need to try. A lot of his work revolves around different communication styles of social justice advocates. Rad, Sad, Mad, Fad, and Glad are his types of advocacy. Our personal attempts to try to make change stem from extreme beliefs that lead to what he calls *Radvocacy*. We may be personally upset or burdened by something that we want to advocate for, making up *Sadvocates* or *Madvocates*. Advocacy of a certain type may be popular or a passing interest leading to *Fadvocacy*. His concept of *Gladvocacy* is to try and engage for the right reasons and claim responsibility for the attempt, successful or not.

"Gladvocacy" Dialogue Principles

1. Declarations of beliefs are not necessarily dialogues about beliefs.

2. The Golden Rule of advocacy dialogue is to be willing to find the truth in what we oppose and the error in what we espouse before we presume to acknowledge the truth in what we espouse and the error in what we oppose.

3. Either-or, all-or-nothing thinking always poses a threat to advocacy dialogue.

4. Gladvocacy dialogue is not without internal contradictions, however, as its basic premises tend to lean leftward toward a liberal-postmodern view of the world (Nash, 101–106).

When taken to this extreme, it is imperative to understand that to be enough is to reflect on one's own lived experiences and determine our habitual behavioral patterns. Keep those we like and focus on those we don't so that we can begin to change what we find necessary to change.

Take a second to list out times that you experienced when an intention didn't follow through with the expected impact. I immediately think of the times when I said something intended to be funny and the joke didn't land. Perhaps the joke had bad timing or involved something inappropriate that I didn't know about.

Maybe I offended someone with a joke that usually others find really funny, but not this time. I have been on both sides of these misses. I have also found myself baffled as to why someone else would make a particular choice. Differently right isn't about being 100 percent right and the other person is 100 percent wrong. This is about leaving room for edits. Take a minute and record times when your intention didn't work out. What was the impact? Then flip it and see if you can determine what someone's intention may have been when you were impacted differently. We are really good at writing stories, so if needed just make up options.

WHEN TO INTERVENE CHART

Your Intent	Their Impact
Tell a funny joke about divorce.	They didn't like the joke because they were just served divorce papers.

Their Intent	Your Impact
Celebrate an honor you received.	The award was long overdue.

Look back over this list. Did you or the other person always have positive intentions with negative impacting results? Could the same happen in negative intentions resulting in positive impacts?

Do the activity again and see if you can identify positive to negative and negative to positive intent vs. impact scenarios.

TEAM LEADERS—
visit www.goodenoughnow.com/freebies for
worksheets, guides, and free fun stuff you can use!

NOTES

INTENT VS. IMPACT SHEET

Your - Intent	Their - Impact
Tell a funny joke about divorce.	They didn't like the joke because they were just served divorce papers.

Their - Intent	Your - Impact
As a warning to not be late again, you are asked to take notes.	You like taking notes because it keeps you focused and feeling important.

Your - Intent	Their - Impact
Grounding a child for the weekend.	They get to miss a school function where they are constantly bullied.

Their - Intent	Your - Impact
Celebrate an honor you received.	The award was long overdue.

SMALL BUSINESS OWNERS—
visit www.goodenoughnow.com/freebies for
worksheets, guides, and free fun stuff you can use!

NOTES

We are all complicated. If we can embrace intention and impact as truths that often are coming from different places, we can truly begin to listen to each other and connect.

We have to leave room for edits for others' lived experiences and learn from these experiences that are different from our own. Just because something hasn't happened to us or doesn't register as a concern or problem doesn't mean it isn't for some. Similarly, something that is celebrated by some isn't by others. To connect, we have to be open to learning about others. To really do this, we have to first be open to learning about ourselves.

"The role of the artist is exactly the same as the role of the lover. If I love you, I have to make you conscious of the things you don't see."
—James Baldwin

Often the intention and resulting impact differ because the players attempting to communicate are coming from different perspectives and lived experiences. Often these differences are also directly linked to our individual identities. Dominant or privileged identities coexist with subordinated or marginalized identities in a given community or culture. Often we advocate from and for community spaces around places of marginalization. This can also be done from places of dominance and privilege. Edwards states that as we develop our identities as aspiring allies, it helps us be more effective, consistent, and sustainable.

Since allies are part of a dominant social group by definition (Broido, 2000), it is helpful to examine the identity development of those with privileged social group identities...we can begin to see how members of various privileged groups might begin to foster a sense of their social group identity influencing the individual's desire and effectiveness working to end oppression (Edwards, 44).

Take a second to make note of your identities and lived experiences and what the counter identity is in our culture.

DIG DEEPER

Subordinated and/or Marginalized

Dominant and/or Privileged

	Race	
	Age	
	Economic class	
	Ability	
	Gender	
	Religion	
	Veteran Status	
	Marital Status	
	Education Access	
	Size	
	Sexual Orientation/ Identity	
	Political Affiliation	
	Nationality	

FRUSTRATING SOMEONE?
visit www.goodenoughnow.com/freebies for
worksheets, guides, and free fun stuff you can use!

NOTES

After completing the chart (feel free to add in others in the blank spaces) circle the identity that you hold in each row. These identities are significant pieces of the story that you have about yourself and the one others write about you. Often these elements are also deeply rooted in the stories we write about others and come with both positive and negative bias. We are responsible for the stories we write and what we do with them. We need to leave room for edits and notice our behavior patterns that impact other people. We can also connect with others around their lived experiences and stories to better our greater community. Pulling from my training participants again, the following are shared learnings in their own words to set an example for the work we must do, redo, and keep doing. Remember, we are enough to try.

Key Lessons: Subordinated Identities and Impact

If we can first identify our subordinated identities and the impact of living while marginalized by others, we can begin to uncover our lived experience and see our patterned behaviors clearer. The impact of others perceiving a piece of us as lesser people also shapes how we think, feel, and build relationships with others.

Often, we form support communities around our subordinated identities, and this helps to heal the intentional and unintentional impact of others, be it silence, pain, or lowered expectations. From these positions of support, it is our responsibility to also bring to light our role in oppression and how we also benefit from our privileged identities that often are forgotten under the weight of real pain.

You may notice in the examples that listing subordinated identities and reporting back the impact they have experienced is much easier than the next activity of listing dominant identities and taking responsibility for one's intent. This reporting of impact leads to shared stories and building support groups or "safe spaces." Perhaps once in these safe spaces, group members could challenge the conversations to reach across shared dominant identities, too.

Subordinated Identity = SI   Impact = IM

SI = *Dual citizen, not white-skinned, female, older, environmentally minded, believer, vegetarian, not born in the U.S.*

IM = *Asked why traveling alone? Why I don't sound Italian? Why don't I consider my parents' current residence home? Being told by other non-whites that I shouldn't feel white guilt. Getting upset when people tell me I'm late (perceptions about my work ethic).*

SI = *Divorced parents, minimal contact with family, alcoholic/abusive family, young, mental health questioned, having to hide my past.*

IM = *When my subordinated identity is challenged, I tend to shut down because it is either a part of myself that I spend time trying to erase as it's a part of myself that I feel afraid of having exposed publicly. I do not like to be seen or treated differently based on an identity.*

SI = *Black-skinned, woman, student, young, incredibly beautiful, dark-skinned, low income.*

IM = *I am more aware of my race and of my differences and I suppose that's what makes me uncomfortable. Anything said about non-whites catches my attention and I notice that when I do notice it, I zone out and either block it out or hypothetically think of racist moments where I would lose control. Because I haven't experienced as many things as a forty-five to fifty-five-year-old, I'm not capable of understanding things the way they do. I am used to being teased a lot about being darker than everyone or just being really dark and because of that I absolutely hate the sun. I've never been comfortable in my own skin and I am angry a lot more than I should be.*

SI = *Gay, lower/working class, no parents, not Christian, young, larger body size.*

IM = *Girls say they want me as their "GBF" to go shopping, gossip, etc., totally stereotyping me as someone I am not. My academic program has very few elective classes. This year one of the electives is replaced by a study abroad course that costs thousands of dollars more. I felt as though I was stripped of an academic opportunity because of my socio-economic class. Whenever someone asks about parents, going home for breaks, or that they must be so proud, it just reminds me of what I have lost and how I'm not like many of my peers. When people thank God for their accomplishments and good standing in life, to me it takes away the pride I have in my personal accomplishments and also allows privileged people to not take responsibility for their privilege: God did it for them.*

SI = *Being American-born Asian, female, introvert, and Facebook protestor.*

IM = *Among "real" Asians, I am inferior in language ability and cultural knowledge. I am frequently told that I speak Chinese very well for being American, and I'm never really sure if this is a compliment or not. I have been racially harassed and the experience has significantly affected me and still does. It's a male-dominated society, and I realized in preschool that I did not* *want to be anything like Barbie or to believe/be any of the stereotypes of women. It had never occurred to me that changing gender might be an option, but I promised myself that, despite being a girl, I never want to be weak or dependent when compared to a male. I also did not want to become obsessive about my appearance or clothing. I find it extremely difficult sometimes to talk in front of a crowd, especially if it calls attention to myself. I tend to speak softly, but I am capable of speaking loudly. I refuse to have a Facebook account. I also don't have Internet access at home.*

SI = *Fraternity member.*

IM = *For the record, I don't often feel subordinated, only rarely. Being in a fraternity means being subordinated by certain groups, even if they aren't dominant. I rarely tell people I've just met that I am in a fraternity because it usually changes the way I'm seen. I had privileged friends that stopped talking to me after an event in another fraternity got their house closed down. People assume I'm an avid date rapist. Even incoming first-year students ask me questions based on perceived stereotypes.*

SI = *Non-white, non-citizen, foreign non-English-speaking parents, poor family, semi-non-able-bodied.*

IM = *I moved to America when I was three years old with parents who did not know a lick of English or American culture. Growing up I was either teased, excluded, or got weird attitudes from friends for not understanding American culture because I felt as though my identity was split in two and forced to keep up with both worlds. On top of that my parents did not make any money, making cultural assimilation harder and worse for me to connect with my friends in the rich suburbs of Boston. This has made me*

*not understand myself for a very large portion of my life so far but
helped me start social justice realizations earlier than my peers.*

What About You? Subordinated (Marginalized) Identities

How have your subordinated identities received impact?

_____

_____

_____

_____

_____

_____

_____

_____

_____

_____

_____

_____

_____

_____

_____

_____

_____

_____

_____

_____

_____

_____

_____

I believe that it is from our dominant or privileged identities that we can best advocate for those oppressed. We also must examine our intentions as well as the unintentional impact of our power dynamics with others.

Being an advocate for others and interrupting intentional or unintentional impact at the hand of often inherited, unearned power is to be an ally instead of a bystander. The risk of advocacy can be real as well as the responsibility to do what is right. It may seem to other dominant group members that there is little to gain by dismantling systems of oppression targeting non-group members, but we must remember that we all suffer together in the light of inequity. Our intentions must come from a genuine place of self-reflection and equity for all. Again, I turn to my clients and their own words from our time working together.

You may notice in the examples that listing dominant identities and taking responsibility for one's intent is more of a challenge for participants than the previous activity of listing subordinated identities and reporting back the impact they have experienced. Ideally, as we get more comfortable naming and claiming our responsibilities for the afforded privileges associated with our perceived dominant and privileged identities, we can use that power to advocate for those who are marginalized, silenced, and oppressed.

Key Lessons: Dominant Identities and Intent

As a straight white male, I often say things that are not intended to be hurtful; however, they still manage to have a negative impact on others. My intent is never to hurt someone. However, because of the triple-threat dominant identity combo of white straight male, I take certain things for granted and my intent is often misleading and ends up pissing a lot of people off.

Oftentimes, I forget how easy I have it. My parents are paying for my college and we have never been worried about paying the bills. Some of my classmates are spending their summers working three jobs trying to make enough money to pay their families' bills and college tuition. I am usually pretty good about being considerate of other people's financial situations or their inability to attend college. I find with these dominant traits I experience a lot of guilt if, say, I spend most of my summer biking and hiking rather than working a full-time job. I also find a lot of guilt telling people where I live because my family has a house right in the middle of town where many wealthy people live. Although my family isn't extremely well off, we were fortunate to find a place there. Although this may seem silly, I feel guilt having an unlimited texting plan. I often assume that others also have an unlimited texting plan as well, when more often than not, they do not.

Just because I have "attractive features" and am pretty, people are more likely to give things my way and I feel that I can get away with more things.

My ex-girlfriend in high school was a year below me and I was going away to college. At that time, we were planning on staying together and I wanted her to be able to go away to college, too. She was very smart and got good grades. However, going to a four-year school was simply not an option for her financially. I remember suggesting to her to get her parents to help her to apply for financial aid because I felt that there must be a way for her to go to school. My intent was genuine, yet it was an interesting experience for me to realize that college is simply not an option for some people. Her whole life she knew that she had to go to the local community college.

College education, healthy, able-bodied, growing up in an urban area, employed, cisgender male, average height, English-speaker, independent—I pay my own bills, U.S. citizen, live in a house—clean water, heat, food, roof, etc., able to travel, able to have different opportunities, access to healthcare.

The intent of asking people/a person about where they are from because they are not white. The intent was to get to know and learn about the person but the impact is the assumption that the person is not from the U.S.

I assume everyone celebrates Christmas because I was raised around that and I accidentally offend people who don't celebrate Christmas.

I honestly think that I tend to get decent grades for handwritten work because my handwriting looks cool. Totally unintentional.

What About You? Dominant (Privileged) Identities

Can you identify dominant identities that informed your intentions?

_____

_____

_____

_____

_____

_____

_____

_____

_____

_____

_____

_____

_____

_____

_____

_____

_____

_____

_____

_____

_____

_____

_____

_____

_____

_____

Key Lessons: Strength in Vulnerability

Vulnerability is the sticky mess that keeps us trapped in our heads, fearing rejection, or paralyzed by not wanting to do the wrong thing. However, it is through our vulnerability and the strength it takes to genuinely share with another authentically that real connections can be formed. Our relationships are as strong as our consistent ability to listen to another, share a moment, and trust both others and ourselves. If we listen to others as if they are wise, we can form a habit that allows us to truly listen to *ourselves* as if we are wise, capable, and able to learn and teach, feel and empathize, and be present in our patterned behaviors and connections.

Examples of strength in vulnerability from my training participants:

"Comfort with being in a state of soupiness or generally emotionally transparent."

Connections and relationships:

"A moment when your weakness is most apparent and a time when you feel uncomfortable often bringing up a past tender experience."

"Exposing yourself to others, maybe showing or opening up to others' weaknesses, relying on others, realizing you can't handle everything on your own, and making yourself open to and reliant upon others."

"Having the strength to admit you need help/support, trust, revealing, builds friendships/relationships, genuine/honest, strength to be/show your true self, helps toward self-awareness."

To be open, let your true feelings show:

"It takes strength to admit you need help/are vulnerable, trust in yourself and others, revealing insecurities, building friendships and relationships, genuine honesty, strength to show your true self and be your true self—work toward self-awareness."

"Authenticity, shame, depth, core, digging, softness, sensitivity."

"Being honest with myself and showing up with all parts of my being—no denial."

"Having strength to share your story without negatively judging yourself. Having pride in your existence no matter how much shame you have carried, and being willing to let new experiences in while receiving them positively."

Reaction/Inaction Patterns

As you reflect, every once in a while turn back and see if you can uncover patterns of your reactions or inactions. When do you respond in a Head-, Heart-, and/or Action-oriented manner? Are there differences in your response behaviors based on what kind of power dynamic is at play? I bet there are! I also bet that depending on your identities and lived experiences there will be patterns there too!

When I used this self-reflection focus in my Intercultural Communications courses at Humboldt State University, I found the emotions and thoughts of my students also fit cleanly into these categories (Head, Heart, Action). Moreover, there are consistent patterns that connect a student's go-to number-one and number-two patterns throughout the semester. In other words, throughout the semester, some students would immediately have a "Head" reaction, and less often or less quickly a "Heart" reaction. In this case, "Head" is their number-one pattern and "Heart" their number-two pattern. "Action" would then be the number-three pattern. What I found was the number-three pattern, whatever that might be, showed up in their final self-reflection quizzes.

Here is an example of these patterns revealed by a student of mine answering the prompt:

What have I learned about myself?

Wow! I guess I've really learned who I am. I've never been a "self-reflector," and thus I've never really thought about who I am. Now, though, I'm starting to understand why self-reflection is so distant to me. It seems that I am a "petty" thinker. This means I like to avoid talks or even thoughts of "deep/insightful/meaningful" stuff. Essentially this is what I have learned about myself—that I avoid philosophical thoughts and conversations. Though this works on the outside, it doesn't fulfill my inner self. As such, I have learned to view myself as an individual thinker. Similarly, since I've successfully gotten inside my head, I can now understand how my general "persona" changes depending on which context I am in. To tie all of this together, I guess what I've learned is that self-reflection doesn't necessarily mean changing my lifestyle. I can think about "Who I really am" without getting all mushy and cliché. I've learned that by not avoiding self-analyzing, I can better understand my own actions. —E. Meslin

Take Space

Taking the time to really sit with one's habitual behaviors, responses, or the lack thereof is the first step toward self-interest and (re)claiming responsibility. If we can know more of who we are, we can sharpen the skills necessary to listen to others' truths. Better listening skills lead to better, more powerful conversations and genuine, lasting connections and relationships. Authentic relationships lead to an extended network of influence that can actually develop systematic change. By knowing one's self, strengthening one's access of influence, it is little or no cost to advocate for others to fully show up. Through advocacy, loyalty, retention, and resourcefulness can take hold.

By working toward social justice, allies are seeking not only to free the oppressed but also to liberate themselves and reconnect to their own full humanity (Freire). Accepting the reality and influence of privilege, allies for social justice see escaping, impeding, amending, redefining, and dismantling systems of oppression as a means of liberating us all (Edwards, 44–49).

No matter what we discover about each other or illuminate in ourselves, we will have life-changing experiences that allow us to lean into our strengths and believe we are not just good, but enough.

FEELING BURNED OUT?—
visit www.goodenoughnow.com/freebies for
worksheets, guides, and free fun stuff you can use!

NOTES

SECTION THREE

NOW

While writing a draft (or many) of this book, I found myself painting our patio chairs on the front lawn. You might have heard the old adage, "a writer's house is the cleanest." What I like about this is that it is procrastination and thinking. There are urban legends of Einstein going for a bike ride to find the error in a problem he was working on. Doing something else can be a distraction as well as a much-needed space to organize one's thoughts and become even more focused. So, there I was painting patio chairs on the front lawn. By distracting my Head- and Action-oriented responses, I gave my heart a chance to feel through the book project and see where I was. A perfect example, of course, appeared.

I had been stalling painting the chairs and couldn't really figure out why. Finally, while applying a coat of paint it dawns on me that

I have been responding to a crucible moment from my past in the present. Back in the 1990s, as a young teen, my father was cleaning up from repainting our home and I took one of the remaining containers of paint to paint the mailbox. Like I had been taught, I circled the mailbox post with newspaper and started painting. The neighborhood bully, Ben Cooksey,[11] and his gaggle of dudes rode past on their bikes and laughed at me for protecting the grass from paint. The grass gets cut regularly, and I had put newspapers down. *Ha ha!* At the time, this was mortifying, and I was really embarrassed to have not made the connection. I stubbornly continued painting with the newspapers in place, and as soon as they all rode by I began crying. Of course, that is when my dad came outside and saw me all snotty and blubbery.

Fast forward thirty-some years, I was spray painting the doghouse, and my husband asked me to put down a drop cloth. (I tend to be a really messy painter.) I was confused because I was on the grass. I felt smart and jokingly said, "But the grass gets cut and will grow back!"

He responded, "Yes. That is true, but the grass right now will not thrive if covered in paint, and the paint can run off into the ground, which is also very bad." I started crying and wasn't sure why. I finished painting the doghouse on the patio out of spite. When painting the patio chairs came up, I was at first hesitant, and then just kept procrastinating the chore. Loren and I were talking about it the other day and he reminded me to put a drop cloth down on the patio or the grass. I felt myself get really angry and quickly changed the subject.

It was in the middle of painting the patio chairs on a drop cloth on the front lawn that I realized that I had responded out of habit. Perhaps writing this book made this easier to see, but I traced my responses back to the boys on bikes. I felt my habitual

---

11   Name has been changed so I don't get bullied as an adult.

response and decided to respond differently. It is my responsibility to take notice of these patterns. At one point, he joined me on the front lawn, and I asked him to point out any spots that I had missed. He hesitantly pointed to one, and I gladly slathered it with paint. I then explained to him that I didn't want to be responding from my past and appreciated him, all that he has taught me about the environment, and how excited I am to sit on the patio with him and watch a sunset. I chose to respond from the present and not out of habit. I chose to respond in the *now* and not in the *then*.

FRUSTRATED BY SOMEONE?—
visit www.goodenoughnow.com/freebies for
worksheets, guides, and free fun stuff you can use!

NOTES

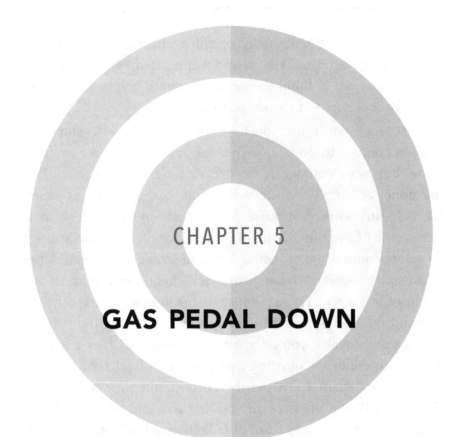

CHAPTER 5

GAS PEDAL DOWN

Taking this self-awareness and responsibility into multiple kinds of conversations and opportunities of engagement with others, we can actually determine how we are likely to show up and adjust accordingly. Once we can embrace our roles in our different relationships and realms of influence, we can gather others who balance our own areas that need support while also supporting others where our strengths are needed. Trusting the pillars of powerful conversations—*curiosity, generosity, vulnerability, and authenticity*—will lend ourselves to being better listeners and develop real lasting connections with others. These real and lasting connections will encourage us and others to show up more and more completely. It is only then that we can retain talent and truly increase innovation and creativity. By fostering an environment of collaboration, it breeds loyalty, resourcefulness, and better use of scarce resources. Intentionally reaching out, listening, planning, and utilizing our Head, Heart, and Action elements allows for all of our initiatives to fulfill the needs of others' habits, leading to a better connection and clearer purpose.

Just when you think you have got it, you have to start over. It takes courage to do your own work and assist others to do the same, but *more* courage is needed to repeat this process. Feeling done, accomplished, or better than someone else is exactly what doesn't work. We must do the best we can with what we have some of the time. Sitting in this space relies on the strength of vulnerability. It takes confidence and strength to create a portal to solicit feedback from customers, clients, and those in your realm of influence. This act must be made habitual for others to respond fully, wholly, and honestly. Once you have the privilege of trust and loyalty, you only increase these variables when you act on this feedback knowing that you are at least trying and are willing to try again. Consistently repeating the process of self-reflection, noticing others as differently right, and leaving room for edits allows for habits to form of reflection, adjustment, and progress. We are all responsible for *who* and *how* we show up all of the time. We are good enough to open the door to real connections and powerful change. We are also good enough, as is, to not have to change everything at once. Let's focus on our strengths, all of our differently right strengths, and support one another in our weaknesses as we evolve and change.

Now what?

"Indeed, acting yourself to a new way of thinking is easier than thinking your way to a new way of acting." —JASON KOTECKI

It is possible that the voices in your head are screaming or maybe whispering sentences that start with *can't, won't,* or *don't.* Please take notice of this. I have been exposed to the concept of "voices in your head" repetitively and from a number of sources. First, my own experience when at the Landmark Forum.[12] I was asked to pay attention to the voices in my head, and I responded, silently, "I don't have voices in my head."

The facilitator looked right at me and said, "You just said something but not out loud. Where does that voice live?"

I responded immediately, "In my head." *Oh,* I thought, *guess I do have voices in my head.* This idea is repeated in the Leader-Shape Inc.™[13] curriculum, in a video of Benjamin Zander. Zander and his partner, Rosamund Stone Zander, co-authored *The Art of Possibility,* which happens to be one of my favorite books. Here again, I am reminded to fully enroll in my actualized life and my responsibility to contribute to others. In reviewing this book again, Zander too attributes the Landmark Forum as an inspiration, as well as William James. While reading my friend Jason Kotecki's book *Penguins Can't Fly,* I also was struck by a William James quote and a take on our inner voices:

> William James, philosopher and psychologist, declared, "Action seems to follow feeling, but really action and feeling go together; and by regulating the action, which is under more direct control of the will, we can indirectly regulate the feeling, which is not." *Indeed, acting yourself to a new way of thinking is easier than thinking your way to a new way of acting.* From now on, instead of acting your age, act more like the person you want to become (Kotecki, 17).

---

12   See http://www.landmarkworldwide.com.

13   LeaderShape, Inc.,™ See https://www.leadershape.org.

Our inner voice is itself the gas pedal necessary to accelerate through crucible moments and become the person we want to be. The real change may be just listening to something we already have direct and free access to. If you internally state that you can't, won't, or don't and believe, yearn, and do it anyway—that is change that will last. Now is the time to do exactly this. Trying is about doing something anyway. Constantly seeking failure allows you to try with equal excitement time and time again. Remember, this is about doing the best you can with what you have some of the time. We are the ones we have been waiting for to do something. We are 100 percent responsible for who, how, and when we show up (or don't) in our relationships, both intentionally and unintentionally. We are responsible for our intentions and the impact of these actions or inactions. We are equally responsible for the impact that we didn't intend. We have two options— hide or try. We hide when we feel unsafe. Feeling unprepared or uncomfortable isn't unsafe. Let's try. Trying will be a learning lesson no matter the outcome. Excitement of achievement doesn't outweigh the fear of failure.

We succeed or learn.

My friend Maura Cullen[14] taught me the concept of "pile up." The idea is that experiences occur and accumulate over time resulting in a response that may or may not seem appropriate at the given time. To understand "pile up" I think we have to also look at all of the other reasons a "can't, won't, don't" voice gets fired up in the first place. Our lived experiences inform all of our future behaviors, decisions, and conscious and unconscious bias. Positive or negative bias affects our habitual responses or lack

---

14   See http://www.mauracullen.com/about-maura-cullen.

thereof. Microaggressions are experienced often and regularly because of this bias and, regardless of intent, can be marginalizing and self-limiting. Internalized oppression is just as real a part of our lived experiences as the experiences of being oppressed by others.

The intersection of these lived experiences may trigger an immediate response that is internalized or expressed outwardly to others, and this may or may not "fit" the situation at hand. If this response is larger, louder, harder than expected it may be due to repeated similar experiences happening over and over again until this breaking point is reached. If you observe this response or this behavioral pattern in someone else, the best response on your part is to genuinely ask questions from a place of care and allow the person space to react and share their lived experience as their truth. If you notice this pattern in your own habitual behaviors, you need to recognize that you are responsible for the intended and unintended impact your personal triggers have on others.

Notice your own patterns. Lean into your strengths and show gratitude for the lived experiences of others that led to the development of these patterns. When you notice something that needs to change, let it go. The root of these patterns can be uncovered, and you can choose to forgive the source. This source may be someone or something from your past or present. The source can also be you and your third-rail element keeping you safe and prepared. This could be your own crucible moment. Listen to yourself and others. Forgive those you need to forgive. Do not expect to be granted forgiveness from those you have wronged. Claim responsibility for these lived experiences and learn from them going forward. It is your third-rail element that both limits and pushes you to grow. Keeping or changing your habits is up to you. It is from here that we can truly become the change we want to see in the world.

Gas Pedal

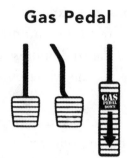

I meet folks all the time who don't know how to drive. You may not be alone, so let me explain briefly and then get back to how our inner voices, or our gas pedal, can both slow us down as well as accelerate our purposeful responses. An automatic vehicle does a lot of the driving for you and only requires a brake and a gas pedal. A standard vehicle involves three pedals—brake, gas pedal, and a clutch. The clutch and the gas work together to shift gears and increase speed or power required on the drive, or this is done automatically. The brake slows a vehicle until it stops and then keeps the car from moving.

You push the gas pedal down to add more fuel and increase speed and you let up to slow down. So if your lived experiences are like driving a car, you have sped up, slowed down, accelerated, come to a screeching halt, and floored it to get somewhere fast. All of the lessons that you have already learned inform how you habitually respond. You have learned what works for you, keeps you safe, and leaves you the most prepared for a given situation. You have taken these experiences and now use them to write the stories about others and situations that you encounter. Leaving room for edits will allow for the stories to become more accurate. Then life happens. The road isn't always wide open and clear, just like there aren't always perfect driving conditions, and don't forget the other drivers on the road. Traffic patterns, construction; is that a sofa in the middle of the road? Life happens. No matter how experienced you are, you fall back to your habits. Sometimes we just need to make new or better habits.

For the same reason pilots practice crash landings, you too retain experiences that took you off guard and they inform future experiences. You will know what to do next time because you learned from other times. This is how your third-rail element works as well. We too have a gas pedal. There are times when we are rocked with excuses and perfectly logical explanations and even rational reasons why we can't respond differently or must not change. This happens to all of us. We also surprise others and ourselves by doing something completely different, even unexpected; it just depends on the situation at hand. We can slow down, coast, or even idle in place. We can also accelerate into a turn, ramp up our velocity, and push through obstacles. It is important to recognize that the gas pedal is exactly what happens during our crucible moments. Our gas pedal makes us good enough.

It takes courage to use the tools that you have at your disposal to make better and more authentic connections with others. Maybe you are already *great* at this, but there is always room to make an improvement. Chances are some connections are solid and others aren't. We all have work to do. Making choices about how you want to show up balances on two elements—risk or cost and reward or goals. There is no downside to responding to a situation where there is no interest in an upside. If we work to habitually make real lasting change in the form of better *authentic connections with generous sharing, vulnerable listening, and genuine curiosity*, we have a goal or reward for our efforts. By truly being all of yourself and allowing others to do the same, there is less of a cost to us all. Perhaps, then, this isn't an act of courage but an act of living.

"It is better to be hated for what you are
than to be loved for what you are not."
—André Gide

Doubting Yourself

It's taken me four years to believe I had something to say enough to even start writing this book. Like Mother Teresa, Gandhi, and Martin Luther King Jr., I get stuck on self-doubt. To gas pedal our way through, we go to our third place—for me, Heart like Gandhi; and for MLK, Head; and Mother Teresa, Action—and we do something different. Interestingly, these are the same places that inform the self-doubt in the first place. Once you find the root, you just do something different and gas pedal through to a new response. I say, "What if I am good enough now?" (Wow, that would be a great title of a book!) Mother Teresa would go serve others when she didn't feel like her work mattered. King would look for systems that connected with his visions.

Negative Thinking

I can't. I suck. I don't know how. I have never done it before. Flip these inside out. *I can. I rock. I can learn. This will be easier next time.* Negative thinking keeps us small. Using the gas pedal here empowers small steps to result in something different. We have all been here. We can all get out of here!

Fear of Failure

My grandmother used to say, "Constantly seek rejection, get used to it, and then you will have nothing to fear." Ask the question; you have a 50 percent chance of getting a different answer than if you hadn't asked. Scientists rejoice in failures because that means they are one step closer to a better solution or outcome. Fearing failure is fearing others' judgment. They are going to judge you even when you succeed. Gas pedal your way through this and recognize when you are letting up on the gas or pressing down. Try. *Vroom vroom!*

Criticizing Others

Judging others is super fun and you can get a sort of high out of being better than someone else. I get it. This is why social media is such a powerful tool. Flip this inside out as well. Our role models eventually learned this lesson too. Judging others without self-reflection doesn't build up others nor is it an effective development tool. What it does is give you the illusion of being better than someone you are standing on top of—being the oppressor isn't a strong goal. Build others up and inspire connections in others.

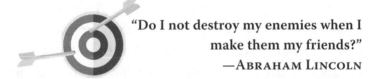

"Do I not destroy my enemies when I make them my friends?"
—ABRAHAM LINCOLN

Negative Self-Talk

This doesn't mean to flip criticizing others into negative self-talk. This doesn't work either. Gandhi would get caught in negative loops of self-talk. These downward spirals didn't help him, his friends or family, or his work. This is a classic example of how our crucible moments and lived experiences get internalized, often without our knowledge, and then we show up like this. We look for negative feedback to validate our self-talk. Look for positive feedback to redirect your self-talk. Use your gas pedal to slow your roll and listen to others if you don't like what you are telling yourself. Seek positive feedback from others until you can give it to yourself. Look, I typed that whole paragraph without a typo! *Woo hoo!*

Procrastination

We talked about putting things off, getting defensive, or deflecting—they really are the same thing just from a Head, Heart, and Action space. Knock it off. Use your lived experiences to push through and try. If you don't have enough gas to do this yourself, fill up your tank by making someone else feel better. Serve others. Practice something you are good at. Press down firmly, and use your third-rail element to accelerate through the situation until it becomes a habit.

Fear of Success

While I am very comfortable with failure, not to mention well practiced, success is terrifying to me. There is a part of me that is convinced that I couldn't ever be successful because I am an alcoholic *and* I have been fired—a lot. This is true and so what? I landed on my feet, have been sober for more than a decade, and thus I am pretty much in line with my biggest role models. Success means I am worthy of not having to struggle always. My identity can't be wrapped up in failure.

My identity is about being resilient and
inspiring others to do the same.
That is success.

People Pleasing

Who doesn't like to be liked? What would happen if we just liked ourself first? This is probably the best example of how our gas pedal can be put to use. If you take all of the other situations out of the picture, it doesn't take courage to do something that the right people like. It also doesn't take courage to keep the wrong people happy. Bystanders, whistleblowers, and you have something in common. We always know the right thing to do. It is the ramifications of doing the right thing that we worry about, and we can't control other people. Honestly, we can barely control our own lives most of the time. Please yourself. Use yourself as the tool to please all of you and others. Use your gas pedal to heal your own wounds to give permission for others to do the same.

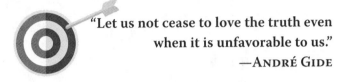

"Let us not cease to love the truth even when it is unfavorable to us."
—ANDRÉ GIDE

What is your go-to excuse? What have you done to keep yourself safe and hidden? What have you done to gas pedal into an uncomfortable experience? What was the result? How does this pattern show up? Why do you choose to keep this habit? How does it serve you and your connections?

Doubting yourself:

_____
_____
_____
_____

Negative thinking:

_____
_____
_____
_____

Fear of failure:

_____
_____
_____
_____

Criticizing others:

_____
_____
_____
_____
_____

Negative self-talk:

_____
_____
_____
_____
_____

Procrastination:

_____
_____
_____
_____
_____

Fear of success:

_____
_____
_____
_____
_____

People pleasing:

_____
_____
_____
_____
_____

Brené Brown states, "I think courage is the ability to tell your story. I've heard so many stories in my life that I know I'm not alone. Everyone has a struggle."

We can't possibly know the struggles that *others* are dealing with unless we make an authentic connection with another, listen as if they are wise with a genuine sense of curiosity, and generously share our own authentic struggles. To do this habitually, we must also do this with ourselves and get out of our own way.

We have discussed how our "go-to" ways of responding are often our strongest assets. We consistently show up with our usual two—Head, Heart, and/or Action—while the third-rail element lies dormant taunting us with excuses, reasons, and habit. To utilize our "gas pedal" we can go around these habits and create new ones in their place. To truly reconcile our being "enough," we need to understand the act of "gas pedaling through," as well as the context in which we can utilize our lived experiences to make real and lasting change in our lives.

Whether reaching out to people in your daily life you haven't really connected with, strangers in the post office line, or *them*—people you have written a story about that has little room for edits—making a powerful connection can open possibilities with anyone, most importantly the possibility of personal growth.

On a recent dog walk, my partner, Loren, a Head-Heart guy, and I, Head-Action, talked about how preparation leads to success and failure. Interestingly, I tend to act and rarely prepare. I will then not start something new because it is likely I will fail. I then have multiple examples of where I tried and succeeded. These successes don't get me through every instance of needing to start a new routine and often just occur. Loren, on the other hand, prepares for everything even if he never uses his preparation. He prepares for longer than anyone I have ever met to increase the likelihood of success. He is more likely to not start something unless he determines that he is properly prepared. When he does in fact act, he tends to be successful. My fear of failure (Heart) and his preparation to act (Action) are then both exhilarating when we apply the gas pedal and take a risk. The reward is the success. Our behavior patterns frustrate and often confuse the other, and with just a little space we can see each other's gas pedal and now motivate and understand the other from their place of need. This is better communication and definitely a better connection.

CHAPTER 6

BETTER

Better communication leads to better connections. To understand how communication works in the first place, we must take a moment to truly understand what occurs during miscommunication and missed connections. We are good enough to connect with ourselves and with others intentionally. We can communicate with our inner voices as well as with those closest to us. We are responsible for who and how we show up even in the briefest of contact with a stranger we will never connect with again.

The authors of *Crucial Conversations* support this notion by describing a powerful connection as:

A discussion between two or more people where (1) stakes are high, (2) opinions vary, and (3) emotions run strong.

Interestingly, the authors continue articulating what we typically do when faced with this kind of engagement opportunity. They write:

We can avoid them.

We can face them and handle them poorly.

We can face them and handle them well (Patterson, 3–4).

After reading too many books on communication, it seems clear that they all agree that there is a minimum of three players in every act of communication. The Sender, Receiver, and Observer, or Third Party. The Sender is the person with the message for the Receiver. The Observer isn't intended to be a part of the conversation but observes it, overhears it, or learns about it. This alone leads to a lot of miscommunications and misconnections.

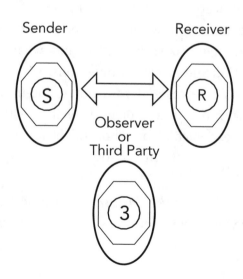

It isn't even this simple. Each player is also a complicated combination of lived experiences, identities, response patterns, and behavioral patterns. Each player has their crucible moments informing his or her inside voice and impacting who and how he or she show up with others.

Lived experiences, crucible moments, and our dominant and subordinated identities	Inside voice and all of our judgments and assumptions	Behavioral patterns, conscious and unconscious, implicit and explicit, positive and negative bias

The communication and conversation books that I have read mostly focus on the outside connections. I posit that these same learning tools can be applied to our inner conversation as well. This cycle must be done intra-personally as well as with those around us to form a habit.

Example: A group I am not involved with but that is associated with a larger organization of which I am an active member had an off-site event where something occurred that was offensive. Person A loved the event and showed a video to Person B who was offended. I learned about the video and the event from third parties. This is how I would fill in the chart.

Person A	You	Person B
Risk/Cost of this connection	**Risk/Cost of this connection**	**Risk/Cost of this connection**
Colleague and friend in the same industry	No risk or cost to me	Colleague and friend in the same industry
Reward/Goal for this connection	**Reward/Goal for this connection**	**Reward/Goal for this connection**
Share a fun moment with a friend as we were discussing the previous evening	Better connections, more fun, better community	Connect with a friend and find out why he was laughing
Background of person	**Background of person**	**Background of person**
White upper-class man with an edgy sense of humor	White upper-class woman with an edgy sense of humor who serves on the board of the larger organization	White upper-class woman with an edgy sense of humor
How does this background inform the message being sent?	**How does this background inform the message being witnessed?**	**How does this background inform the message being received?**
He found this event outrageously entertaining	The fine line between edgy humor, community building and sexism that exists in the organization	Unprofessional, not collegial, out of context, shocking, irresponsible
What is the intention of this communication?	**What is the intention of this communication?**	**What is the intention of this communication?**
Share humor and a laugh	Minimize shock and shame or guilt of an over-share that didn't go well	Connect to a friend and find out about an event they didn't attend
How did this person listen during the conversation?	**How did you listen during both processing conversations?**	**How did this person listen during the conversation?**
Didn't. Shut down and got mad. Reached out to women who attended the event to find out why friend was being so sensitive. They didn't mind, why does she?	Anxious, but tried hard to get both sides of the conversation. Unsure of proper protocol as a new board member. Reviewing own experiences of being targeted by sexism.	Didn't. Shut down and got mad and reached out to other women to find out what the context was and what should be done if anything about the event. Wants immediate punitive response.

Person A	You	Person B
What meaning was made from the impact of the miscommunication?	**What meaning was made from the impact of the miscommunication?**	**What meaning was made from the impact of the miscommunication?**
This particular woman is too sensitive.	Sexism is rampant and, as a woman, I don't know if I can do anything about it even from a position of power.	Critical of the larger organization and demanding disciplinary action for the event while naming that this is a pattern of sexism in the organization.
How does this impact their connection?	**How does this impact their connection?**	**How does this impact their connection?**
Blown off as a sensitivity justified by other women's support.	Builds frustration in that I can't fix the incident or the larger issue at hand.	The end of a collegial friendship.
How did they claim (or dismiss/deflect) responsibility for this impact?	**Do you have any responsibility as the third party to this misconnection?**	**How did they claim (or dismiss/deflect) responsibility for this impact?**
Total dismissal as an isolated incident and oversensitivity.	Be available to listen while also uncovering a pattern of sexist experiences I have had and those that I have colluded with in the past.	She took responsibility for having an edgy humor and relationship that may have let Person A feel like it was okay to share the video in the first place.
How is the connection now?	**How is the connection now?**	**How is the connection now?**
None.	Same but more anxiety until the first contact with both occurred.	None.

Take a moment and draft out a miscommunication that you witnessed. You get extra *unicorn points* (!!!) if you pick a conversation where you know what each party intended and how this misconnection impacted the other person.

Person A	You	Person B
Risk/Cost of this connection	*Risk/Cost of this connection*	*Risk/Cost of this connection*
Reward/Goal for this connection	*Reward/Goal for this connection*	*Reward/Goal for this connection*
Background of person	*Background of person*	*Background of person*
How does this background inform the message being sent?	*How does this background inform the message being witnessed?*	*How does this background inform the message being received?*
What is the intention of this communication?	*What is the intention of this communication?*	*What is the intention of this communication?*

Person A	You	Person B
How did this person listen during the conversation?	How did you listen during both processing conversations?	How did this person listen during the conversation?
What meaning was made from the impact of the miscommunication?	What meaning was made from the impact of the miscommunication?	What meaning was made from the impact of the miscommunication?
How does this impact their connection?	How does this impact their connection?	How does this impact their connection?
How did they claim (or dismiss/deflect) responsibility for this impact?	Do you have any responsibility as the third party to this misconnection?	How did they claim (or dismiss/deflect) responsibility for this impact?
How is the connection now?	How is the connection now?	How is the connection now?

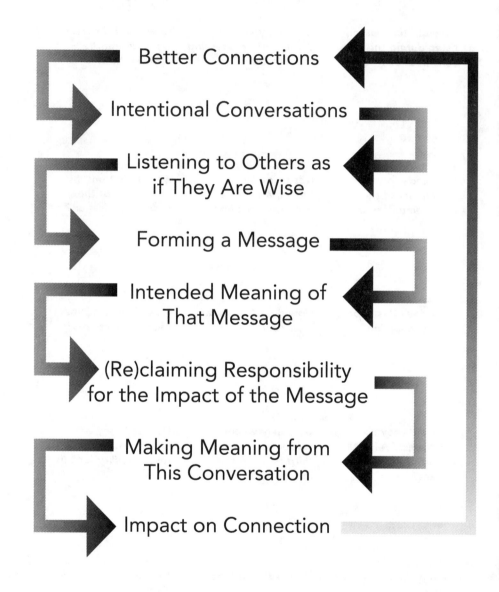

Better Connections

We have people in our life who have survived a lot of time with us. The history alone makes them connections for life. Our closest circle of connections can weather a lot of storms. Missed connections aren't just for strangers, colleagues, co-workers, and the like. I have lost some of my closest friends because of a pileup of miscommunications on either my part or theirs resulting in the end of a relationship. Romantic breakups, moving, losing jobs, the end of a volunteer role, or some other kind of significant life change can impair our connections with one another. We have to take responsibility for the connection we had, have, and will make. Doing self-work is about connecting, reconnecting, and making a better connection with our own lived experiences and habitual behavioral responses. All connections are powerful or can be. Powerful connections are the key to showing up and allowing others to do the same. In *Social Excellence*, this is a three-step process—simple, but not easy (Mattson, 162).

1. Choose to engage.

2. Choose to care.

3. Choose vulnerability.

To purposefully make our connections better, we have the choice to intentionally enter into a conversation, listen with empathy, form our messages with full understanding of our backgrounds and lived experiences and how that informs our communications, claim our responsibility for our intentions and the impact of our messages, and fully acknowledge that each exchange can lead to better connections.

Intentional Conversations

There are lots of models and theories on how to communicate better. Instead of overwhelming you with options, I think it is important to focus on what informs our intentions and take responsibility for the impact of our messages. If you want to dive deeper, here is a quick overview, taken from "Models of Communication" as adapted from *The Magic of Dialogue* by Daniel Yankelovich and the *Beyond War Study Series*,[15] of all the ways we often communicate or connect with others.

- Nonviolent communication

- Clean communication

- Cooperative communication

- Centered communication

Interestingly, these models focus on the building blocks of external dialogue between Person A and Person B. Being intentional is key and this intentionality must also build better connections between our own histories and how this informs who and how we show up in conversation as well as make meaning from messages we receive while not being intended receivers.

 "Listen to others as if they are wise."

Listening to Others as if They Are Wise

I got a fortune cookie once that said, *"Listen to others as if they are wise."* I often tell a story about when this first really

---

15   See http://beyondwarnw.org.

made sense to me. I was on a walk with a dear friend's young son, Neil. They live in a rural area of Vermont, and we were walking maybe an hour or so deep into a forested area, not seemingly following a trail of any kind. He delighted in showing me fiddleheads and edible berries, different tree leaves, bugs, and the like. At some point, I got worried that we were lost and that it would be dark before we got back to the house. I don't see well at night and really don't like being lost, so as the dusk insects increased their presence my anxiety did as well. I mentioned to Neil that I really was getting worried about being too far away from home a number of times, until he seemed to notice that I really needed to get home and took off running. I panicked and ran after him. We ran maybe 100 yards and were back at the house. We had been walking in a circular pattern and hadn't really ever gotten that far from the house. It is also important to mention that he has done this walk every day of his life. I just didn't trust him. I didn't listen to him as if he had any information that I didn't. I was lost. He was right at home.

What I learned that day, what Neil taught me is the importance of a *better connection*. To truly have a better connection, I have to employ my Head, Heart, and Action elements so that I can show up not just as a listener but as a genuinely curious, authentic, generous, and vulnerable person (Heen, 7–9). By not focusing on the transcript or words being exchanged, I can "forget the words" and focus on the authenticity of the moment. While I was experiencing being lost in the woods of Vermont in the dark, I missed moments of sheer glee that I could have shared with Neil.

Are you familiar with your inside voice? I like to make a joke and point out that if you answered that question, likely it wasn't out loud. You used an inner voice. We do this all that time. This inside voice is imperative to acknowledge within us. It is with this voice that we make all judgments and assumptions that then inform our behaviors. My demeanor shifted in the woods with Neil whether I meant it to happen or not. I reentered his home a self-deprecating little girl. I am certain I must have acted like that somehow. This is the difference between intent and impact. I didn't intend to freak out or validate a theory Neil is forming about adult behavior. I wanted to get home before dark and didn't trust Neil to take care of me, and that impacted our ability to connect. This isn't complicated, but it can be difficult. The solution isn't easy, but it is simple.

 "Adults are weird and worry instead of wonder."

For better connections to happen, I need to converse from a "stance of curiosity" by listening from the inside out (Heen, 167). My internal voice was having its own conversation. I was desperate to know how far we were from the house and started feeling panicked and frustrated that I had set myself up to be reliant on a five-year-old, which then sent me directly to my third-rail element of excuses and self-limiting beliefs. I then found myself entering an internal conversation about yet another of the world's precious and magical gifts of a found animal track with the mindset of why do I fail to plan ahead. Two different conversations are taking place. I am no longer able to truly listen to the young boy's discoveries or nature lessons, and I find myself in a self-talk spiral of a little girl who should have known better. Successful connection and relationship building cannot be built on this as a foundation. I am responsible for this. This, of course, wasn't my intention. Curiously, I wondered what impact my internal voice had on the little boy's excursion. After I calmed down a bit, I talked with Neil about how I doubted his sense of direction and asked him what it was like for him.

Neil quickly responded, *"Adults are weird and worry instead of wonder."*

Maureen Linker, in her book *Intellectual Empathy*, explains listening and our roles as listeners as:

> Becoming better listeners. This might seem...very passive...but listening can be very active. In addition, listening the right way can be a component of moral action. Philosopher Miranda Fricker, in *Epistemic Injustice*, uses the phrase "virtuous hearing" to describe the habit of listening with a "reflexive critical awareness" to correct for "prejudice in our judgments of credibility" (Linker, 180).

Our lived experiences can directly impact our ability to listen, form messages, make meaning, and truly connect with one another. This bias, positive or negative, can be used to intentionally make better connections. We just have to try.

Gene Knudsen Hoffman, Leah Green, and Cynthia Monroe's *Seven Challenges Workbook*[16] developed a concept called *compassionate listening*. Compassionate listening weaves together empathy, intention, and listening. Here is how they say to do this:

- Consider how you would feel if you were in the other person's shoes.
- Start with positive intentions.
- Listen to their side and take time to let it sink in before reacting.
- Consider their needs and feelings.
- Address them respectfully.

I would also add, make a conscious note of the lived experience differences and similarities Person A and Person B have with

---

16   See http://www.NewConversations.net.

one another. Our crucible moments inform all of our messages and our capacity to truly and better connect with another person. Linker continues with:

> Active virtuous listening would mean that we pay attention to the experiences of people with social identities and experiences different from our own while also considering the following kinds of questions:
>
> - What biases and preconceptions might be affecting how I listen to this person (or group)?
>
> - Am I rushing to the judgment that this person is not telling the truth, that the person is exaggerating her or his experiences or misunderstands those experiences?
>
> - Do I feel defensive (and world erasing)?
>
> - Is it hard for me to adopt a playful attitude of loving perception because I am tense, anxious, or uncomfortable? (Linker, 180)

Intentionally providing space for a better connection allows for both you and the other person in the conversation to show up fully. We can choose to see them as differently right and leave room for edits. We can take each connection and move one step further and internally process the exchange so that we can better connect with ourselves, the person, and others again. To better connect, we must listen to others and our inner voices as if they are wise.

Forming a Message

No matter how much room you leave for edits or give yourself or others space to be differently right, we are still responsible for forming a message in the first place. We get to choose what kind of message we want to send as much as how we are going to receive a communication. The manner in which we do this is deeply rooted in our habitual behavior patterns.

I recently shared a picture via text message with my dear friend Sylvie. The text I got back read, "Great picture! Who is this?" I received a text back from a number that I had saved as Sylvia in my cell phone. I did a double take because the only Sylvia I know is my Aunt Sylvia who passed away a few years ago. My first response was to question why this stranger has my aunt's cell phone. I took a minute before responding and realized that Sylvia's number had been recycled. I also realized that I typed Sylvia instead of Sylvie when I sent the original picture. I then responded to the person with my aunt's former number, "Sorry for my mistake. I meant this for someone else. You have my aunt's cell number. She was a wonderful person. I bet you are too. Glad you liked the picture." They responded with something like they loved the idea of having a cell number with a positive history and were here if I ever just needed to text my aunt.

I chose in that moment to re-form my response, and it resulted in a better connection. Following all of the communication training that I have gone through, I made sure that I used positive "I" messages that also didn't blame the other person for not knowing they had my aunt's number. I also relaxed my shoulders, shifted the tone of voice, even if it was just inside of my own head, and typed a text with the intention of having a better connection than just a mistake text. I resent the picture to my friend Sylvie. By intentionally forming a better message, I made at least three better connections.

1. To my Aunt Sylvia and my memory of our relationship.

2. My friend Sylvie who loved the story about the stranger.

3.   The stranger who never knew the history of their cell number...and now even more as they share and you, the reader, share.

Forming a message with your full self in mind matters. To allow space for others to fully show up, we must allow space for our full self to show up. This means the good, bad, ugly, and awesome parts of ourself are just as important as the elements of the person you want to connect with.

Intended Meaning of That Message

In the *Fifth Discipline Fieldbook*, Rick Ross discusses *skillful discussion* and reaching a decision mindfully. "People 'discuss' to win. They have ideas against each other, as Bill Isaacs puts it, to see whose ideas will be the strongest." The "go around" idea here is spot on, in that, to reach the "best ideas and solutions" we need to host better discussions with one another. Moving from raw debate to polite discussion is where most tough conversations seem to occur. With a habit of self-reflection and ownership of one's own responsibility in a conversation, we too can learn a "go around" and have better conversations.

Ross continues with a list of protocols to have better and more *skillful discussions.*

1.   Pay attention to your intentions.

2.   Balance advocacy with inquiry.

3.   Build shared meaning.

4.   Use self-awareness as a resource.

5.   Explore impasses (Ross, 385–391).

This "go around" idea pairs nicely with the concept of using your gas pedal to stay engaged in a discussion to lead to better connections. Pay attention and notice your own meanings as they are informing the intention behind your messages. Don't passively listen, but engage, ask questions, leave room for the other person to share and connect with you too. Your self-awareness will role model the space for the other person to share from an authentic place. Being curious with your intentions and exchanging messages in a generous manner will not eradicate miscommunication, misunderstanding, or disagreement, but it will allow for these elements to not stifle, destroy, or end a better connection opportunity.

I would also add, give yourself a break. Remember, we are shooting for some of the time as well as just doing the best you can with what you have. As you enter a really challenging conversation or turn to a contentious relationship, step into the connection with the future in mind. Use your third-rail element to develop possibilities of what might be going on with the other person. What are some possibilities of their reaction? Try really hard not to aim or set them up for a particular response. Having fewer expectations of the connection outcome or the other person's role in a conversation allows your focus to be on you and how you show up in the moment (Heen, 122–126).

We are never entitled to a response or engagement. We do get to protect ourself, feel safe, lean on others for help, and process with others. We are responsible for the patterns or ingredients needed to develop into feelings of danger. Once aware of where these feelings come from, we decide intentionally if we want to keep this response pattern or change it. Regardless, it is our authentic purpose to reflect on this interaction for the next connection opportunity. It is through this reflection that allows you to share your views and feelings as well as lived experience with others so that they have a chance to connect and share with you their authentic story. Your generously listening to them sharing their story creates more opportunities to powerfully connect that will increase the amount of support each party feels, leading to a deeper connection and building fertile ground for collaboration, innovation, and teamwork (Heen, 145–147).

(Re)claiming Responsibility for the Impact of the Message

Intentionally having better connections is super simple, but not easy. (Re)claiming responsibility for only the things you can control is super simple, but not easy. In *Difficult Conversations*, Heen, Patton, and Scott break this struggle into three things that you must accept about yourself:

1. You will make mistakes.

2. Your intentions are complex.

3. You have contributed to the problem.[17]

Our actions have to support our connections. We must leave room for edits in our preconceived stories while listening and take in more accurate information from the other person. Remember, we can all be differently right. If in the moment we can suspend our final drafts, we can leave room for a truthful exchange and focus on learning about each other. By holding genuine curiosity with generous advocacy, we can support our dialogue intentionally, even if at the car wash, grocery store, work, or at the dinner table. In *Fierce Conversations*, Susan Scott asks a key question, "What are you pretending not to know?" (Scott, 70). Missed connections happen when we aren't showing up to a conversation authentically. What is there about you, the message, or the other person that I pretend to not know exists? We cannot pretend pieces of our lived experience don't show up or have been resolved. We carry our histories with us in every conversation, and they lay the foundation of all of our connections.

---

17   Heen, 119–121.

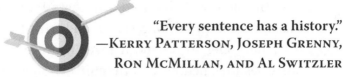

"Every sentence has a history."
—KERRY PATTERSON, JOSEPH GRENNY,
RON McMILLAN, AND AL SWITZLER

Consider this: Successful relationships require that all parties view getting their core needs met as being legitimate. You won't articulate your needs to yourself, much less to your work team or life partner, until and unless you see getting your needs met as a reasonable expectation. So pry the permission door open just far enough to consider that you have a right to clarify your position, state your view of reality, and ask for what you want. Coming out from behind yourself is part of the search, whether born of panic or courage, for that highly personalized rapture of feeling completely yourself, happy in your own skin. It is a reach for authenticity—a process of individuation—when you cease to compare yourself with others and choose, instead, to live *your* life. It is an opportunity to raise the bar on the experience of your life. It is a deepening of integrity—when who you are and what you live are brought into alignment. No more damping down your soul's deepest longings in order to get approval from others. ...The principle job at hand is to intertwine addressing your current business and personal issues with self-exploration and personal development, building a bridge between yourself as a person and yourself as a professional (Scott, 72–73).

Making better connections with others is only half of the work. We also need to turn these tools inward and really become more self-aware. In connecting with our habitual behavior patterns and having a more truthful sense of self, we can discover, or perhaps uncover, we are truly enough as is.

> It is through such humbling insights into ourselves
> that we come to know, reshape, and trust the self we
> may then offer to others. It takes courage to look at
> ourselves unflinchingly in the mirror called our lives.
> Sometimes what we see isn't particularly attractive. It
> has been said that the truth will set you free—but first
> it may thoroughly irritate you! (Scott, 75)

When turning these skills to our dominant or privileged identities and lived experiences, we won't just be irritated per se, but we
may also go through stages of defensiveness, guilt, shame, paralysis,
numbness, etc. We are responsible for these responses as well. The
responses are more than likely rooted in your third-rail element,
and with self-awareness you can gas pedal your way through it.

Debby Irving writes about her journey as a white woman
coming to terms with her whiteness, white privilege, and doing
anti-racism work. It is just as much of a self-awareness journey as
the struggle she fights with each connection.

> The powerlessness and isolation I felt as a bystander
> (which I didn't even realize I was) have been replaced by
> a sense of empowerment that comes with feeling there's
> a critical role for me in dismantling racism. But here's
> the catch: it's trickier than one would think to take on
> the role of an ally and not be, well, too white. I should
> not be in the role to take over, dominate, or be an expert.
> The role is not for me to swoop in and "fix." The whole
> ally role is a supporting one, not a leading one.
>
> I also have to be careful not to replace the idea that "I'm
> a good person" with "I'm a good ally" and therefore think
> I am not susceptible to screwing up and don't need guid-
> ance from people of color and other white allies. I will
> always have to check my privilege, my perceptions, and
> my behaviors as I try to work in alliance with people of

all colors in the struggle to interrupt, advocate, and educate. Much like pursuing good physical health, working to be an effective ally means making a commitment and working on it. It seems just as I think I've got it, a racialized current event or interpersonal exchange reminds me just how much I need to seek perspective and support from others who understand the dynamics of racism. It's a lifelong commitment (Irving, 220–221).

> Interestingly, it is my gas pedal that can be my vaccine (habits), kryptonite (excuses), and antidote (being good enough now).

As stated before, this work is never over. Just focus on doing the best you can with what you have some of the time. I promise this is better than nothing, and what you bring to these connections and conversations or interactions is enough. In her book about personal retreats, *Unwrapped*, Laurie Guest states, "This is the day of reckoning. It is the time when I am called to account for my actions and fulfill my promises to myself" (Guest, 149). Making promises for real change for others is one battle that I grapple with. Keeping promises I have made to myself is a whole other war with all of my habits, self-limiting beliefs, and excuses.

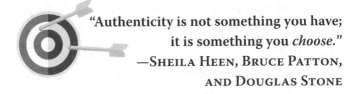

"Authenticity is not something you have; it is something you *choose*."
—SHEILA HEEN, BRUCE PATTON, AND DOUGLAS STONE

Making Meaning from This Conversation

Clarity is needed to form a message in the first place, but we often forget that in claiming our own sense of responsibility we must be clear with what we do with the process of mean-ing-making as well. We may only receive a small portion of the messages in the manner in which they were intended. These messages could be observed, picked up secondhand, or delivered in a direct conversation. It is up to us to take these messages in as they were intended and to notice the patterns of our responses as we make meaning. Often, others will try to tell us of patterns that we don't even notice. We get feedback all the time, and if we make any meaning of it, it is typically from a place of defense or deflected back to the sender of the message. If we leave room for edits in our own stories, we can take in new messages and receive the intended meanings as edits. Again, turning to Gene Knudsen Hoffman, Leah Green, and Cynthia Monroe's *Seven Challenges Workbook*,[18] the act of making *message meaning* comes in three parts:

- Be clear.

- Be as open and honest about your feelings and needs as possible.

- Focus on strengths and positive characteristics more than weaknesses.

By creating a safe space based on curiosity, vulnerability, generosity, and authenticity, trust can build and better discussion can begin to regularly occur without a facilitator. If new ideas are given space to develop, conversations can grow and include more people while also having a structure for the discussion so topics can stay grounded and focused. Listening is really key to getting around our "go-to excuses." Listening to ourselves, *others'* feedback, and *others'* stories and experiences is a must. To best listen, stop talking. Stop voicing both inside and outside of your own head and take in the messages around you. Look for patterns,

18   See http://www.NewConversations.net.

nonverbal messages, validation or contradiction from others, and watch the flow of the conversation. Being open to a conversation that you haven't written the script for and cannot edit while it is happening allows you to engage in a whole new way. This may be overwhelming at first, so tell one person and get help. Ask for one person to pay attention to how you "show up" in conversations. Take their feedback as helpful no matter what patterns they notice.

Practice...breathe...reflect...
learn...repeat.

Our lived experiences, self-reflections, personal retreat time, and our own development of self-awareness lend themselves to this exchange of histories with one another. Everything about who, how, and where we are and who, how, and where we have been passes between each person we choose to engage with and even those we don't.

Our own positive and negative conscious and unconscious biases are at the root of our ability, or lack thereof, to make edits to our own story. To edit the story we have about ourself, we often have to rely on those closest to us for feedback and then really take responsibility for these patterns. Remember, we can keep the ones we like and only need to focus on those that we want to change. Maureen Linker, in *Intellectual Empathy*, lists "Questions to Counter the Effects of Cognitive Biases." She explains:

> We should pay careful attention to whether the biases are operating in our own arguments and the arguments presented by others…. The prevalence of these biases should put the following questions at the forefront of our thinking and reasoning about issues related to social difference:

- When I explain my problems and the problems facing people like me do I attribute those problems to external conditions rather than to my own behavior? And when I explain the problems facing people who are not like me, do I attribute those problems to their behavior rather than external conditions?

- Do I prefer the people who are like me in circumstances where identity becomes the issue? Do I have the tendency to take a stronger position than I would normally when I believe that people like me are under attack? Do I believe that people like me are much more reasonable and varied in their opinions about our social group and that those who are not like me are much more rigid and extreme?

- Do I prefer that things remain the way they are in terms of race, ethnicity, religion, sexual orientation, dis/ability, and immigrant rights because changes will bring about worse conditions for me (and people like me)?

- Am I confident in my social beliefs because most everyone I care about and spend time with shares these beliefs (rather than because I have actually challenged or tested them by seeking evidence outside of my family and friends)?

- Do I pay attention to media reports that I judge to be unfair to me and people like me and ignore those that I believe to be in favor of other groups?

By carefully keeping these questions in mind and paying attention to how we take in and process information, we can reduce the effects of cognitive biases in our beliefs about social differences (Linker, 120–121).

For one to hold responsibility for their own bias, empathy for our own and others' histories, and a genuine sense of virtue in our conversations takes practice, patience, and, André Gide would emphasize, courage.

What comes to mind with these prompts? How does your lived experience and conscious and unconscious bias, both positive and negative, impact your meaning-making? Can you intentionally use these experiences for more accurate meaning-making? How do you respond from the present moment versus from habit?

Use this space to take notes.

When I explain my problems and the problems facing people like me, do I attribute those problems to external conditions rather that to my own behavior? And when I explain the problems facing people who are not like me, do I attribute those problems to their behavior rather than external conditions?	
Do I prefer the people who are like me in circumstances where identity becomes the issue? Do I have the tendency to take a stronger position than I would normally when I believe that people like me are under attack? Do I believe that people like me are much more reasonable and varied in their opinions about our social group and that those who are not like me are much more rigid and extreme?	

Do I prefer that things remain the way they are in terms of race, ethnicity, religion, sexual orientation, dis/ability, and immigrant rights because changes will bring about worse conditions for me (and people like me)?	
Am I confident in my social beliefs because most everyone I care about and spend time with shares these beliefs (rather than because I have actually challenged or tested them by seeking evidence outside of my family and friends)?	
Do I pay attention to media reports that I judge to be unfair to me and people like me and ignore those that I believe to be in favor of other groups?	

Impact on Connection

I often hear over and over again that I am perceived to be fearless. It is habitual for me to deflect this away largely because I am anxious and so debilitated by my own fears that it is hard to understand how I could be brave or courageous. Over time, I have come to terms with the fact that when I fear something, I usually proceed ahead and try. Often the reward or goal outweighs the risk or cost of the very thing that is causing my fear, so I step forward. This act has become a pattern in my own life and now a habit. Courage to be all of my imperfect self as often as possible is brave because it comes with risk and at a cost of insecurity, failure, and reprimand. The reward is being true to myself while (re)claiming responsibility for all that is in my control.

With every conversation, we have the opportunity to make a better connection. The impact of a connection is all that we have to really make better connections. When thinking about conversations that are often contentious or fearful, we can start by looking at our lived experience and then leave space for someone else to have a very different experience than we included in our draft story. When dialoguing across differences, no matter our intention, the impact of our messages is our responsibility. For example, Singleton and Linton define a *courageous conversation about race* as "utilizing the agreements, conditions, and compass to engage, sustain, and deepen interracial dialogue about race in order to examine schooling and improve student achievement." Specifically, a *courageous conversation*:

- *Engages* those who won't talk.

- *Sustains* the conversation when it gets uncomfortable or diverted.

- *Deepens* the conversation to the point where authentic understanding and meaningful actions occur.[19]

For the best impact, we must commit fully to leaving room for edits and holding space for each conversation partner to show

---

19   Singleton and Linton, 16.

up differently right. We can aim for our intentions to match the impact of a conversation if we provide space for discomfort, truth, and intentional engagement. We are not entitled to being right and shouldn't enter into a conversation expecting to win or lose. All connection partners will have a better connection when they expect to show up fully and allow space for others to do the same.

This is true for all kinds of connections to be better, whether talking about race, class, ability, politics, or any form of communication across difference. Pulling from Singleton and Linton's "Six Conditions of Courageous Conversations" (Singleton and Linton, 18–19), conversation partners must take into consideration the identities and lived experiences of both players. Ideally, this needs to be "personal, local, and immediate" and not theoretical or metaphorical in nature. Connect lived experience to lived experience and not in theory. To really hear an unintended impact your messages may have had, we have to stay focused and be clear on what we are trying to talk about. Better connections come from sticking to the subject at hand and not bringing in other variables or distractions. Having a "broad scope" conversation can lead to a pileup effect that becomes more of a challenge to engage with or respond to. Form a message focused on one clear element and present that in conversation for the best connection with another person.

Of course, there may be other contributing factors to the problem being discussed, and that leads to a richer connection. Being open to this broader scope allows the other person to share, and you can ask questions about their experience. This experience paired with yours and others that you have connected with adds value to every connection. They are all authentic lived experiences. Another form of impact of a better connection is a clearer understanding of vocabulary, acronyms, variables, symbols, and systems connected to the topic at hand. Being open to new, shared, and differing uses of terminology allows for all conversation partners to teach and learn from one another for as long as each partner wishes to participate. We are not guaranteed closure or a declared winner. Nor does a given conversation have a set start, middle, or end. A better connection can pick up, pause, and pick back up again without a clear end. When receiving feedback or engaging in a better connection, be mindful of how your own lived experience and behavioral patterns show up in conversation regardless of the others involved. Taking responsibility for these patterns is the best way to have better connections. It is truly the most generous response we can have when someone is being vulnerable with us to return the favor and accept this as their truth, as if it is a gift. There is no better connection than this.

To take this concept one step further, if we do the best we can with what we have some of the time, we are likely on our way to being able to have what Susan Scott calls a *fierce conversation*, or "one in which we come out from behind ourselves into the conversation and make it real" (Scott, 7). *Fierce conversations* also follow the same pattern of being Good Enough Now. Scott introduces her concept of *fierce conversations* with these seven principles:

1. Master the courage to interrogate reality.

2. Come out from behind yourself into the conversation and make it real.

3. Be here, prepared to be nowhere else.

4. Tackle your toughest challenge today.

5. Obey your instincts.

6. Take responsibility for your emotional wake.

7. Let silence do the heavy lifting.[20]

---

20   Scott, xv–xvi.

Remember, this is messy work that never ends. As soon as you make progress, you must continue to dig and find more pieces to examine, take responsibility for, celebrate, and share with others. These truths about your own lived experience are the best and strongest tools you have to share with others. This is what makes you and your authentic self a valuable connection for others. It is this never-ending non-linear process that pairs listening with self-reflection and the claiming of responsibility that results in better connections with your own sense of self and with others. Heen, Patton, and Stone introduce the concept of "difficult conversations" in a book of the same name by taking the emphasis off of a clean step-by-step process and focusing more on looking in your own right place for the answers. They write, "What can we suggest that you haven't already thought of? Probably quite a bit. Because the question isn't whether you've been looking hard enough for the 'answer' to difficult conversations, it's whether you've been looking in the right places. At heart, the problem isn't in your actions; it's in your thinking. So long as you focus only on what to *do* differently in difficult conversations, you will fail to break new ground."

If we do the best we can with what we have some of the time, we always have "enough" to try to engage authentically with one another. What is paramount is, even when we engage and it goes badly or we avoid the connection all together, we are responsible for these choices, patterns of behavior, and our own histories that led us to show up this way. Our own histories and behavioral habits can be faced and handled well or poorly, but they can't be avoided.

In *Crucial Conversations: Tools for Talking When Stakes Are High*, Patterson, Grenny, McMillan, and Switzler write:

> The Law of Crucial Conversations: At the heart of almost all chronic problems in our organizations, our

teams, and our relationships lie crucial conversations— ones that we're either not holding or not holding well. Twenty years of research involving more than 100,000 people reveals that the key skill of effective leaders, teammates, parents, and loved ones is the capacity to skillfully address emotionally and politically risky issues. Period (Patterson, 9–10).

Research has shown that companies with employees who are skilled at crucial conversations:

- Respond five times faster to financial downturns and make budget adjustments far more intelligently than less-skilled peers (Research Study: Financial Agility).

- Are two-thirds more likely to avoid injury and death due to unsafe conditions (Research Study: Silent Danger).

- Save over $1,500 and an eight-hour workday for every crucial conversation employees hold rather than avoid (Research Study: The Costs of Conflict Avoidance).

- Substantially increase trust and reduce transaction costs in virtual work teams. Those who can't handle their crucial conversations suffer in thirteen different ways (backstabbing, gossip, undermining, passive aggression, etc.) as much as three times more often in virtual teams than in collocated teams (Research Study: Long-Distance Loathing).

- Influence change in colleagues who are bullying, conniving, dishonest, or incompetent. When nearly 1,000 respondents were asked, 93 percent of them said that, in their organization, people like this are almost "untouchable"—staying in their position four years or longer without being held accountable (Research Study: Corporate Untouchables).[21]

If we are both *good* and *enough*, what do we do now? Now, we reclaim our gas pedal and do better. We take ahold of our responsibility for who and how we show up and make more authentic connections with one another. This will make us unstoppable.

---

21   Patterson, 12–13.

CHAPTER 7

HOLDING SPACE

Recognizing that we all have different lived experiences that make us who we are and how we are with each other—this is a lifetime of work by itself. Understanding how systems of oppression exist, and how we all both benefit and are marginalized by these very systems may be easier from our subordinated positions and must be understood from our more dominant positions as well. This work leads us to understanding our conscious and unconscious bias as well as uncovering the roots of our habitual response behaviors. Moreover, we can use this information to articulate our Head, Heart, and Action response patterns in which there are two elements that we most often turn to. This leaves identifying our third-rail element so that we can silence the voices fueling our excuses and self-limiting beliefs and then gas pedal or accelerate us through crucible moments in our life. This practice will become a habit and allow us to hold space for connection with others that matter. Holding space is the answer.

To best explain, I am going to turn to the 1984 classic movie *Ghostbusters*. You may not remember this movie or have it queued up for emergencies in iTunes like me, but there is one principle I want to borrow. In the movie, there are proton packs the Ghostbusters wear on their backs to attack or confine a target. Throughout the movie, it is imperative that the Ghostbusters *do not cross the streams!* The scientists are not sure what will happen, they just assume it is bad, until the end of the movie (spoiler alert) where crossing the streams actually saves the day.

I suggested that we go Ghostbusters style and cross three streams of what seem like unrelated aspects of our culture and our habitual interactions with one another. We must cross the streams, do something different, to get a different result. It is a tall order, and I believe, after more than fifteen years of working with people inside systems to uncover problems and illuminate tactics to lead to better results, the answer is in the combination of these three heavy topics.

 We must cross the streams, do something different, to get a different result.

- First Stream: Take responsibility for your own lived experiences and who and how you show up as well as the stories you write about others.

- Second Stream: Recognize that others are complicated and have survived a lot to be standing with you and therefore are worthy of the benefit of the doubt.

- Third Stream: Claiming the opportunity to have conversations that matter is the only way better connections will be made.

If these three streams are crossed, the result is the concept of Good Enough Now.

First Stream: Take responsibility for your own lived experiences and who and how you show up as well as the stories you write about others.

Determining that we are innately *good* is the first step. We can be released from perfection and try anyway. Believing that one is *enough* is in itself revolutionary. To be *enough*, we must understand how our lived experiences inform our habitual responses and behaviors first. Then and only then can we really hear someone else's lived experience and see how that informs their way of being in the world and in relationships. There are a lot of books that talk about listening to others and adjusting how you show up to meet their needs for better success in making a connection. Developing a sense of empathy isn't manipulative once it is rooted in curiosity, generosity, vulnerability, and authenticity. Building loyalty, increasing innovation, retaining talent, recruiting better, and showcasing your strengths can only be done when the streams are crossed. What better way to increase engagement than creating and fostering space for self-motivated people to fully show up with all of their strengths and in full awareness of their weaknesses? Once we can all be fully present, new ideas, resourcefulness, community, collaboration, and extra efforts become a given. Only *now* can a team that feels *good enough* lean into progress, change, and teamwork. This is applicable in social movements, politics, family life, business strategies, and the like.

This is where, why, and how this book is being written, so that we can collectively arrive with our full-lived experience, good, bad, ugly, and awesome, and together we can make real lasting change with confidence and energy. We have to build or hold this space intentionally, because we don't get it through our education or socialization processes in school. Tim Wise writes in *White Like Me*, "History textbooks and literature reading lists of schools all around the nation...they look exactly as they did twenty years ago; mostly white folks' narratives, with a smattering of 'others' more as an add-on than as a central part of understanding this nation and its collective story" (Wise, 16). Surely, with constant research being conducted and new literature being produced every year, new materials, edits, and stories could be included, but they aren't. It is difficult to understand why (Head) more inclusive reading lists can't be widely used in our school system (Action) so that all students can learn and benefit from the broadest education possible (Heart). This isn't a new problem.

Leaving space for someone else to be
good enough is revolutionary.

Second Stream: Recognize that others are complicated and have survived a lot to be standing with you and therefore are worthy of the benefit of the doubt.

Difficult topics are usually just complicated situations. "It's complicated" is fine for a Facebook relationship status, but we don't typically like it anywhere else. Combine a complicated situation with an unspeakable topic, and we typically get even less progress. I remember finding Wise's book in a discount bin at a bookstore when I was in graduate school. His words helped me feel responsible:

> By owning our collaboration we can regularly see our own shortcomings, place them within the larger context of our culture's subsidizing of those shortcomings,

and then commit ourselves to doing better next time. The most dangerous person is the one who refuses to admit that he does in fact contribute to injustice at least as often, if not more so than he truly rebels against it (Wise, 102).

Feeling a part of the problem is how I got out of my own way and started making and seeing real change in my own life.

Historically, most difficult topics in our current society aren't new. Even if we take something like cyberbullying, this isn't a new topic but a new method of an age-old problem—people being mean to others—often leading to the same wide range of outcomes from being ignored or feeling like an outsider to something significantly more dramatic like revenge, death, suicide, mass shootings, or genocide.

"It's complicated" isn't an answer but an excuse to distance ourselves from taking responsibility to really look at what is happening. If we go to Facebook relationship statuses, "It's complicated" may describe a multi-partner relationship; the lack of a desire to even desire a romantic, emotional, or sexual relationship; or somehow try to encapsulate the point in a relationship that is just starting or just ending, and much more. Typically, when I see a friend change their status, I reach out to see if they need a listening ear. Sometimes this reach out is truly out of support and genuine curiosity, and other times it is motivated by my need to know or gossip. Polyamorous and asexual individuals may not have a lot of support or space to really share who and how they are in the world, just like folks starting or perhaps ending a relationship may not know who or how to describe what is happening.

We understand complications, difficulties, and unspeakable elements of our own and others' relationships.

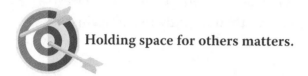

Holding space for others matters.

We can use this same skill set when we think about people being differently right. I tend to gravitate to controversial topics that aren't welcome at the dinner table as a way of demystifying the complications. I will do this here for two reasons: 1) explaining things through something else difficult makes other applications seem easier, and 2) all problems are solved by taking individual responsibility, listening, and being our full selves to do the best we can with what we have some of the time.

Third Stream: Claiming the opportunity to have conversations that matter is the only way better connections will be made.

> There are ways to talk to people, even truly tough cases, and make some headway, break down some defenses, get people to at last begin to question the thing they have always taken for granted precisely because they have never been challenged before by anyone who looked like them.... You can't organize people if you don't love them (Wise, 90).

If there is a system built on groups having powers that other groups don't, then the "up" group is dependent on the "down" group. This dependence usually shows up as a lack of understanding, noticing, believing, seeing, or even acknowledging any lived experience different in the "down" group, leading to the subordination, silencing, and marginalization of members perceived to be a part of this other group. Moreover, the "up" or dominant group is made up of other groups "more up" or more privileged so we can collectively feel like we are without something that some-one has and would have to give up something for someone else to have something. This system is dependent on others being 1) self-reflective, 2) paying attention to the greater system, and 3) lis-tening to others' truths as valid and not as competition.

> Broido (2000) built on earlier definitions (Wash-ington & Evans, 1991) to define social justice allies as "members of dominant social groups (e.g., men, whites, heterosexuals) who are working to end the system of oppression that gives them greater privilege and power based on their social-group member-ship" (p. 3). Allies engage in social justice efforts to reform or dismantle systems of oppression and strive towards a "vision of society in which the distribution of resources is equitable and all members are physi-cally and psychologically safe and secure" (Bell, 1997, p. 3) (Edwards, 41).

In order for this to actually manifest, I posit that the only way to effectively dismantle an inequitable system is to claim (or reclaim) responsibility for our individual ways of being. Our individual ways of being are often from both dominant and sub-ordinated positions inside of this system.

"When you're accustomed to privilege, equality feels like oppression."
—AFRO PUNK MEME

Our suffering is equal to that of others. Our joy is equal to that of others. This is what it means to hold space for a genuine connection.

Instead, what happens is we, individually and collectively, get comfortable in the problematic system and see that others are setting rules for us to abide by so we approach one another guarded, defensive, and not our full selves. If our full self isn't present in our relationships, at work, or in the grocery store confronting a stranger, we feel less and less inclined to take responsibility for our habitual behavior pattern because it is only a part of us that behaved in a certain way to begin with.

Early in the first several pages of the book *Difficult Conversations*, the authors map out four types of conversations: 1) what happened conversations, 2) feeling conversations, 3) identity conversations, and 4) learning conversations. Where the person or persons in a conversation are determines what kind of conversation may be taking place or, more importantly, being perceived by each conversation partner as actually happening. I would also add that these types of conversations can happen one on one, in groups, and internally. I don't think the complexity of conversation is fully understood in a Sender/Receiver diagram, and I appreciate the allowance for conversations to be difficult. Part of this difficulty, in my opinion, is the lack of awareness of how each voice is showing up time and time again in any conversation and where these habits are formed out of protection and defense.

A *what happened conversation* may be more Head response than others in that facts are being sought. Perceptions can vary through individuals' lived experiences, so knowing the intentions and the impact of a given conversation can be complicated, leading to a Heart response of, "How could you say that?" or "How could you hear that?" The *feeling conversation* may default to a Heart response, but this is often when someone wants to be heard and see exactly why someone is feeling the way they do and inform the next action. The Head piece of a *feeling conversation* can be an asset and a hindrance. What the authors refer to as an *identity conversation* seems to encapsulate a particular story that one of the conversation players needs to hold on to and/or share with others. The story we have about ourselves comes directly from our lived experiences and can be true sharing and personal disclosure as much as the story can be a habitual excuse or particular lens in which the conversation partner sees a skewed or limited reality. Ideally, if all conversation partners (including what may be multiple inner voices) can fully show up to express themselves and be wholly received, supported, and heard, we would have a *learning conversation*. To truly listen and share with others, we would undoubtedly learn more about one another and ourselves.

At a recent speaking engagement, an audience member asked me about holding space being weird. He asked, "If I want to connect with someone, but they haven't heard this message, won't it be weird?" I responded that entering a conversation with a brochure of definitions and connection models would be weirder. With each conversation attempt, with yourself and with others, you enter a connection with a sense of curiosity and ask genuine questions anticipating learning something. We must listen to the other as if they are wise and try to learn something. When we hold space there is little to no expectation connected to the outcome. This is a good kind of weird. Leaving yourself open to hold a conversation without sacrificing a piece of yourself is good weird.

C. Jones and K. Shorter-Gooden surveyed a number of black and African American women about the need or expectation to "shift" with each held social role to retain a sense of safety and preparation. These shifts come at a great cost to an individual's ability to show up.

> Once you're used to living in a hostile environment and you get good at it, and you understand the rules, it's hard to let down your guard.... At first it sounds kind of powerful, like "It doesn't really matter what happens to me—what's important is how I respond." And I remember thinking "Oh, that's good stuff." And then I thought "that is so unhealthy!" ...How painful

to realize how over time I had lost my ability to feel in the moment. It's like, "I don't have the luxury of being scared right now. I need to figure out how I'm going to get out of this situation. I can be scared later" (Jones and Shorter-Gooden, 79).

As your internal voice begins to kick in, I am not suggesting to ignore it but to listen closely to it. This voice or these voices have been with you your whole life. Much like the woman interviewed in *Shifting* realizing that her hostile work environment was preventing her from feeling or being healthy, our inner voice guides us and navigates us through rules we perceive to be in place. Ideally, we need to actively embrace our inner conversations to unlock the patterns of our behavior. Once we can notice how we show up, only then can we decide what we want to keep and what we want to change. A genuine sense of curiosity, generosity, authenticity, and vulnerability can lead to significantly more powerful conversations. These conversations can be with others as well as with our selves.

Powerful conversations are defined by choosing to engage, care, and be vulnerable in *Social Excellence: We Dare You* (Mattson, 162). Curiosity, generosity, authenticity, and vulnerability are the four pillars of their dare to be socially excellent. Moreover, they define this journey as starting with *desire* building up the *gumption* to start *communicating* and make a *connection* and *relate* to others. This leads to better *networking* and *association* with others for meaningful *engagement* and *influence*. Once empowered with influence, *societal relevance* and *social significance* can occur (Mattson, 188–189).

This is good stuff!

I do feel the need to remind you that we are shooting for some of the time with what you already have. Remember, this isn't a model of explicit answers. I see, far too often, folks who wield models, knowledge, and vocabulary like a weapon in conversations with others. There is not enough room for more cape-bearers and sword-carriers. I do not present this information as a tool for "gotcha moments" for you to attack someone else or to discipline yourself for unsavory behaviors. This is simple and complex. We are all a part of this complicated system, and the art of conversation—listening to connect, sharing to relate, and reclaiming responsibility—is the antidote. It is good enough now.

Considering the Conversation: A Documentary on a Taboo Subject is a film about hospice care and end-of-life conversations. A researcher speaks of an older woman whom she had seen over a period of time and never appeared to have any friends or family visitors since she arrived into hospice: "If this woman had fifteen minutes to really speak her mind to her family—what would she say? 'I fear being a burden,' or 'I fear pain.' Would she list things that can be left undone? Can't be left undone?" The problem is fifteen minutes prior to her losing her ability to speak, she didn't know that was her last 15 minutes of speech. At the last visit, did she know this is the last visit?

I often reflect on this scene and think about the things I didn't know. The last delightful meal cooked together and shared with a now ex-lover. The last run with a healthy, happy dog before illness and age caught up to us. The last visit with a long-time close friend before they moved away. I don't think it is realistic to live my life or hold every conversation as if it is going to be my last one with every living being that I come in contact with. Sometimes, I really don't want to talk at all. What I learned from the dying woman in the hospice care documentary is the concept of islands of excellence. What if for everyone, once in a while, I was excellent? This excellence may be self-serving or it could be for someone else. One of my favorite quotes by none other than Dolly Parton herself is, "If you see someone without a smile, give 'em yours. You can make more." Islands of excellence could be orchestrated by me and kept track of like a scorecard, but I would miss all of the excellent moments I shared with others without noticing. This is why a paradigm shift is required to change our habits so that the intended and unintended impact of our behavior patterns can truly be a reflection of our whole selves whether we are conscious or not.

I am lucky enough to be able to call Tim Wise a friend now. I can reach out to him and not have to find him in a book bin at a second-hand store like I did twenty years ago. Interestingly, our conversations are still about the same issues as if they were front-page headlines in the news. Not a lot has changed in multiple difficult topics both outside of us and inside of us. I believe that if I can semi-consistently work on my own self-reflection I can claim responsibility for who and how I am in the world. This is my life's work.

 Society will change for the better when we individually do our own work.

> [We] can't escape [power and privilege] until the society is fundamentally changed. But we can opt for resistance. We can refuse to cooperate. We won't always do it perfectly; or even well; it often won't be easy. But it is necessary, and if we refuse to do it, we are indeed collaborating with things the way they are. In the face of injustice, one can either try to throw the gears in reverse, or continue inexorably downhill, in which direction surely lies tragedy (Wise, 94).

The truth is that we need strategists, activists, and passionate people to collaborate and work together even if at first glance they seem to be on opposite sides of an issue. What we are currently doing isn't increasing the amount of joy anyone is experiencing. The wealthiest members of our society seem miserable. Children are suffering from hunger, poor education, and a lack of stability at home more so than ever. Even animals are suffering from weather and traffic changes that make it harder to thrive.

 I put up with whatever cost I have to put up with, because the cost of not doing the work is greater.

—TIM WISE

What if real, lasting change didn't cost anything and didn't require anything new? It seems worth a shot to try. I have found in my own life, and after a decade or so of education and training others, that the simple act of looking inward, instead of for an answer to be developed, created, bought, or built, is working better. Perhaps this is a higher cost because it is rooted in self-awareness and taking responsibility for things that are a problem for others. Just because it isn't a problem for you, doesn't mean it isn't a problem. Perhaps that is the highest cost of all—real connection from real listening to one's self and others. I find that there isn't anything working well yet. I also find that the work I have done with my own Head, Heart, and Action behavioral patterns has led to significant change in my relationships with others and my own self-development. Perhaps it is worth a shot?

How did we get good enough? Why do we care? These are key questions if we are going to give this a shot. If we can move forward acknowledging there is a difficult topic or complex problem that needs to be resolved—in our relationships, at work, or in the world—ultimately it comes down to a simple problem of perspective. As long as we can point a finger away from us, the problem lies outside of us. What if this is the paradigm shift required for real and lasting change? I am not suggesting that all problems lie within us, but perhaps the answers do.

We all write stories about others. We don't like to call these judgments and assumptions, but that is what they are. Most of us have been told a thousand times that making judgments and assumptions is *terrible*, but we do it all the time. Instead of trying to never ever make them in the first place, what if we just work with the judgments and assumptions we do make and build from there? We actually make judgments and assumptions for at least two really good reasons: 1) to be safe, and 2) to be prepared. It is our lived experiences that inform how and when to write these habitual stories, and this is the piece that needs to be reclaimed. If we can take responsibility for the writing of stories that may or may not be completely accurate, then we can still feel safe and prepared and then listen to others to edit our story with more accurate information in each case. I call this leaving room for edits. Go ahead, write your story, even better if you can identify the patterns of these stories and identify their sourcing information. Print that story out triple-spaced with extra-wide margins and then genuinely engage in a conversation with the person who is the target of the story and seek edits. By asking questions rooted in genuine curiosity and listening to the other person's actual experiences, you can edit your original story like a draft for accuracy. The skill set of wanting to be right is already in place here. We just need to leave room for edits to get "righter," so that we don't have to be defensive or feel wrong. This is the foundation of powerful conversations.

Paying attention to your stance when you get defensive is important. When do you react this way? Is there a pattern? When are you less likely to get defensive even if the ingredients are there, but seem to be less challenged to listening and taking in new information? Same thing goes when we think about when we do or don't intervene, procrastinate or initiate, make excuses, or try. We must acknowledge that our lived experiences make us who we are and how we are in this life. To look at race, racism, and white privilege as an example, Frances Kendall writes:

As white people, we have to believe that we can change ourselves and our institutions. Without that belief, the system of the supremacy of whiteness continues to work exactly as it was set up to work, and all of our lives are lessened. In its own way, each of the crucible experiences I have identified taught me to look at complexities, and each provided me the opportunity to become more deeply committed to work toward a world in which authentic relationships across race not only can happen but can thrive. My belief is that this is where white people have to begin—by looking at ourselves. Through that personal work, we become clearer about the necessity of changing our institutions, and we work to build a greater repertoire of skills to make the needed changes (Kendall, 18).

Cultivating self-interest is dangerously close to being self-absorbed. I would guess that these skill sets are in the same grocery aisle, yet are very different from one another. Being self-absorbed in the day and age of selfies, instant gratification, and immediacy is a statement of our lack of connection with one another. I was recently in Jamaica for a service trip and engaged with another volunteer about why she takes so many pictures. She was just as curious why I don't. I don't bring my phone because I want to be present. She takes pictures to remember. I am not sure that either is ideal and neither is self-absorbed. The volunteer who complained to me that the shells, starfish, and rocks hurt her feet less than an hour after we worked on building a house for a mother and her three children is self-absorbed. Both hold one's self at the center of the conversation, but there is different intent.

The power that the "up" or dominant group is privileged to be given may appear to be selfish, but these privileges come at a cost too. The "down" or subordinated groups of people often have to be more self-interested for survival, but need to also be self-reflective. Typically, each individual has both "up" and "down" experiences in their lives, and it is evidence that the current system harms all that are concerned. We must reflect on how we got where we are and at what cost to ourself and to others, and work toward real, lasting change to benefit all.

> Although privileges as a result of hierarchical and oppressive systems are very real and may appear to only benefit members of the dominant group, ultimately the system of oppression also harms those from the privileged group as well (Brod, 1987; Freire, 1972/2000). For example, as a result of individual and societal homophobia a heterosexual man may find it difficult to form meaningful interpersonal relationships with gays and lesbians. On a deeper level, members of dominant groups may suffer a loss of authenticity and humanity as a result of their unearned privilege and dominant position in society (Freire, 1972/2000). Brod (1987) argues that members of the dominant groups are so deeply harmed by their often-unwitting participation in a system of oppression, that they would ultimately be better off without the unearned privileges resulting from the system of oppression. Although there are many reasons members of dominant groups seek to dismantle the systems that grant them this unearned privilege, breaking free from this pain and becoming "a worker in your own liberation" (Bishop, 2002, p. 100), is a key step in becoming an effective, consistent, and sustainable ally (Edwards, 43–44).

To be an ally is to understand one's realm of influence and how we came about with the access that we in fact already have. This isn't a one-time process, but a lifelong process of (re)claiming responsibility, gaining awareness, and being open to new experiences and lessons shared by others.

"I am regularly asked by people of color, 'Why would white people begin to look at themselves and their privilege? What would motivate them to move out of their comfort zone?' My response is a work in progress" (Kendall, 20). It is by holding space for these connections that we make progress.

NOTES

CHAPTER 8

GOOD ENOUGH NOW

Changing habits is a whole other section of the bookstore. Ultimately, we all know how to change a habit. Scott "Q." Marcus, of This Time I Mean It,[22] has developed a list of Commandments of Changing Habits that rings as true as it makes me chuckle.

- Thou art complete from the beginning.

- Thy life is thine own creation.

- Thou shalt enjoy the benefits of thy habits.

- Listen not to the pressure of others...

- ...Yet accept thy journey is not alone.

---

22   See http://thistimeimeanit.com/handout. Use password "handout" for full listing.

- Thou shalt accept time is out of thy control.

- Give unto thyself more credit.

- Thou shalt be free from long-term binders.

- Expect not guarantees of success.

- Thou shalt think smaller.

- Don't expect what you expected.

This is how to do the best you can with what you have some of the time. Also, in changing habits, it will take you reaching out to others for feedback, support, guidance, and encouragement. Moreover, this is an ongoing process. When you lose weight, it is also about how long you can keep the weight off, always and forever. I quit drinking over ten years ago; I am still an alcoholic. The struggle to be while developing into who I want to become is doing real self-work. No one else can do this work for me. Self-awareness can't be outsourced, delegated, or shipped overseas. This is all you. I can be where I came from while being present and under construction.

"Ego says, 'Once everything falls into place, I'll feel peace.' Spirit says, 'Find your peace, and then everything will fall into place.'"
—MARIANNE WILLIAMSON

Fall of 2019, the entering first-year college students will be the first college class where 9/11 is a historical event that occurred prior to their birth. When I first moved to New York City in 2002, I would ask for directions and be told in reference to where the towers once were. I never saw them. Now, the new tower is a skyline reference point. All of these elements are true. We can hold our lived experience with the current moment while focusing on our future selves. We can discover who and how we are, be with people as we are now, and do better.

Often we think or feel that once *we* have something we can *do* something more effectively and then and only then we can be something we yearn to *be*. Flipping this upside down is real lasting change. We must *be* who we yearn to *be*. Being this person allows us to *do* something more effectively so that we can ultimately *have* something we don't currently possess. Our life starts with taking responsibility for our being and how we show up, why we habitually respond the way we do, and where our greatest strengths can best support others and vice versa.

Dr. Chérie Carter-Scott, MCC, developed a list of *Ten Rules for Being Human* in her book *If Life is a Game, These Are the Rules*, which are as follows:

1. You will receive a body. You may like it or hate it, but it's yours to keep for the entire period.

2. You will learn lessons. You are enrolled in a full-time informal school called "life."

3. There are no mistakes, only lessons. Growth is a process of trial, error, and experimentation. The "failed" experiments are as much a part of the process as the experiments that ultimately "work."

4. Lessons are repeated until they are learned. A lesson will be presented to you in various forms until you have learned it. When you have learned it, you can go on to the next lesson.

5. Learning lessons does not end. There's no part of life that doesn't contain its lessons. If you're alive, that means there are still lessons to be learned.

6. "There" is no better a place than "here." When your "there" has become a "here," you will simply obtain another "there" that will again look better than "here."

7. Other people are merely mirrors of you. You cannot love or hate something about another person unless it reflects to you something you love or hate about yourself.

8. What you make of your life is up to you. You have all the tools and resources you need. What you do with them is up to you. The choice is yours.

9. Your answers lie within you. The answers to life's questions lie within you. All you need to do is look, listen, and trust.

10. You will forget all of this.

This last rule is the key. "You will forget all of this." Nothing here is new. There are dozens of books referenced, cited, and recommended here that have very similar messages. The key reason this concept keeps getting reexamined, packaged differently, and presented anew is that we consistently are looking outside of ourselves for answers when the answer is in us and has been in us all along. We are the best tool we have to make change. If we only have total control of ourself some of the time, then it follows that some of the time we could do the best we can with what we already have to make real lasting change. Does this leave you feeling overwhelmed? Good. Notice this. And try something different anyway. Sure, it would have been *great* to do something differently long ago, but we didn't. We are left with today, right now. The pressure of tomorrow is enough to stop me in my tracks. The promise of tomorrow is enough to keep me going.

 "The best time to plant a tree is twenty years ago. The second best time is now."
—CHINESE PROVERB

And now, I turn back to William James. In 1899, James gave a speech, "Talks to Teachers on Psychology: And to Students on Some of Life's Ideas," and parts of this speech were republished as *On Vital Reserves: The Energies of Men; The Gospel of Relaxation.* It is in this speech that I feel my ideas articulated here come full circle, lest we forget again.

James starts with the assumption that we don't typically operate in full all of the time. We show up our less than full selves due to lack of interest, low energy, boredom, and habit. "Excitement, ideas, and efforts, in a word, are what carry us over the dam" (James, 13). Then once we reach this tipping point, we eventually become comfortable again at this new point and push the "dam" further off until there is yet another tipping point. Similarly, thrill seekers and those who turn to drug use or self-harm often artificially create these tipping point moments, to break out of a fatigued habit and "reanimate" or feel alive again (James, 24). Yoga or some kind of regular exercise routine may be slowly integrated into one's life until it becomes a habit, and then something different and new will need to be added to continue to elevate one's full self, even though we still don't often show up or use 100 percent of our energies. New experiences or ideas unlock "what would otherwise be unused reservoirs of individual power" (James, 29). "Whatever it is, it may be a high-water mark of energy, in which 'noes,' once impossible, are easy, and in which a new range of 'yeses' gains the right of way" (James, 34) "Part of the imperfect vitality under which we labor can thus be easily explained. One part of our minds dams up—even damns up!—the other parts" (James, 37).

"Conscience makes cowards of us all."
—WILLIAM JAMES

When turning these concepts to our relationships, engagement opportunities, and impact on others, James continues to explain how we can keep pushing the "dam" further and further out while building better connections with others.

> One hearty laugh together will bring enemies into a closer communion of heart than hours spent on both sides in inward wrestling with the mental demon of uncharitable feeling. To wrestle with a bad feeling only pins our attention on it, and keeps it still fastened in the mind: whereas, if we act as if from some better feeling, the old bad feeling soon folds its tent like an Arab, and silently steals away (James, 46).

Nomadic stereotypes aside, James is drawing our attention to what I hear more commonly now as, "fake it until you make it."

Interestingly, James's concept of "bottled lightning" is similar to my third rail concept. Remember, our friends like us anyway; perhaps they see the good of our gas pedal while we may more often experience the excuses from the same variable.

The idea that how one is may or may not correlate with how one acts is also supported by James, referencing Freud's *Binnenleben*, our "inner atmosphere in which one's consciousness dwells alone with the secret of its prison-house," in that others may observe a certain truth about how something is that the person themselves may not see. "This inner personal tone is what we can't communicate or describe articulately to others; but the wraith and ghost of it, so to speak, are often what our friends and intimates feel as our most characteristic quality" (James, 48). This "bottled lightning" concept is really how we show up and others experience whether we are aware or even intentionally being a certain way (James, 56).

James's *Gospel of Relaxation* is really pivotal here. Knowing what you know now, this process of self-reflection cannot be done 100 percent of the time on full blast immediately. You cannot mass produce nor efficiently stumble upon your own "bottled lightning."

> It is your relaxed and easy worker, who is in no hurry, and quite thoughtless most of the while of consequences, who is your efficient worker; and tension and anxiety, and present and future, all mixed up together in our mind at once, are the surest drags upon steady progress and hindrances to our success (James, 63).

This comes to mind the clearest when I think of what I call Social Justice Warriors or cape-wearing PC (political correctness) Police. If you bring an egocentric sense of entitlement and condescension to a conversation, you will shut it down instead of foster it. One cannot be generous when listening to another if you are in full-tilt judgment mode and looking for confrontation all of the time. Moreover, your attempts to educate someone else of the wrongdoing without evidence of self-reflection, self-awareness, and empathy lead to completely ineffectual results. However, if you relax into these conversations and genuinely engage and listen with curiosity and vulnerability to foster an authentic exchange of knowledge, both parties can feel progress. Everyone wants to be heard. No one wants to feel stupid. Pulling from James again:

> We must change ourselves from a race that admires jerk and snap for their own sakes, and looks down upon low voices and quiet ways as dull, to one that, on the contrary, has calm for its ideal, and for their own sakes loves harmony, dignity, and ease. ...And, if you

should individually achieve calmness and harmony in your own person, you may depend upon it that a wave of imitation will spread from you, as surely as the circles spread outward when a stone is dropped into a lake. ...If one's example of easy and calm ways is to be effectively contagious, one feels by instinct that the less voluntarily one aims at getting imitated, the more unconscious one keeps in the matter, the more likely one is to succeed. Become the imitable thing, and you may then discharge your minds of all responsibility for the imitation. The laws of social nature will take care of that result (James, 65–67).

"Become the imitable thing."
—WILLIAM JAMES

Recently a friend, Mike, told me a story about his soon-to-be stepdaughter, Zoe. From his perspective, Zoe is as tenacious as she is resilient, and to watch her develop before his eyes is his favorite part of being a new parent figure. Just as I was putting the final touches on the final draft of this book, one of his stories came just in time. While at a ropes course at a campsite, Zoe and her mother took on a multi-level challenge course. Just as Mike's partner reached the third or fourth level (about four stories in the air), Zoe was struggling to get to the second level. Zoe stopped and went back to the first level, deflated and disappointed. She turned around and saw her mother crest the top of the fourth level and progress to the fifth. In that instant, Zoe turned and figured out how to get over to the second level and kept climbing. Mike said, "It isn't just that she tried; it is that she never quit trying to try."

Can you do that? *Never quit trying to try.*

For real change to ever happen, we will, we must do something different. Real lasting change in our relationships, both personal and professional, starts with our (re)claiming responsibility for how we show up. We are the best tool we have access to for the purpose of building something different. If we start individually, I deeply believe that others will join us and follow. Collectively we can role model the way into the unknown—the different—so we don't have to go at this alone. The mindset or paradigm shift necessary is that our own work is what is needed to truly role model for others the space for their whole lived experience to be present. We must hold on to connections between our shared experiences and with genuine curiosity listen to our different perspectives and lived experiences. Opportunities for powerful conversations and generous contribution to one another's growth on fertile ground are made from the spaces of authentic sharing and our vulnerable strengths. Our ability to be differently right allows us to see each other as the solution or resources that we in fact cannot bring to a particular problem. At the root, while doing the best we can with what we have some of the time, we must leave room for edits about ourselves and "them."

We are Good Enough Now.

BIBLIOGRAPHY AND SUGGESTED RESOURCES

Adams, Maurianne, Lee Anne Bell, and Pat Griffin. *Teaching for Diversity and Social Justice: A Sourcebook.* New York, NY: Routledge, 1997.

Alessandra, Anthony J., and Michael J. O'Connor. *The Platinum Rule: Discover the Four Basic Business Personalities—and How They Can Lead You to Success.* New York: Warner Books, 1996.

Allport, Gordon W. *The Nature of Prejudice: The Classic Study of the Roots of Discrimination.* New York, NY: Basic Books, 1979.

Anderson, Sharon K., and Valerie A. Middleton. *Explorations in Diversity: Examining Privilege.* Belmont, CA: Brooks/Cole, 2011.

Anti-Defamation League. "Pyramid of Hate." Adl.org. 1998. Accessed November 14, 2016. http://www.adl.org/assets/pdf/ educationoutreach/Pyramid-of-Hate.pdf.

Avolio, Bruce J., and William L. Gardner. *Authentic Leadership Development: Getting to the Root of Positive Forms of Leadership.* Amsterdam: Elsevier, 2005.

Bennis, W. G., and R. J. Thomas. "Crucibles of Leadership." *Harvard Business Review* 80, no. 9 (2002): 39–45.

Berkowitz, A.D. *Applications of Social Norms Theory to Other Health and Social Justice Issues* in H. Wesley Perkins. *The Social Norms Approach to Preventing School and College Age Substance Abuse: A Handbook for Educators, Counselors, and Clinicians.* San Francisco: Jossey-Bass, 2003.

Bishop, Anne. *Becoming an Ally: Breaking the Cycle of Oppression in People.* London: Zed Books, 2002.

Brod, H. *A Case for Men's Studies* in Michael S. Kimmel. *Changing Men: New Directions in Research on Men and Masculinity.* Newbury Park, CA: Sage Publications, 1987.

Broido, Ellen M. "The Development of Social Justice Allies during College: A Phenomenological Investigation." *Journal of College Student Development* 41 (2000): 3–17.

Brown, Brené. *Daring Greatly: How the Courage to Be Vulnerable Transforms the Way We Live, Love, Parent, and Lead.* New York, NY: Gotham Books, 2012.

Cameron, Julia. *The Artist's Way: A Spiritual Path to Higher Creativity.* Los Angeles, CA: Jeremy P. Tarcher/Perigee, 1992.

Cameron, Julia. *Walking in This World: The Practical Art of Creativity.* New York: J.P. Tarcher/Putnam, 2002.

Carter-Scott, Chérie. *If Life Is a Game, These Are the Rules: Ten Rules for Being Human, as Introduced in Chicken Soup for the Soul.* New York: Broadway Books, 1998. www.drcherie.com.

Considering the Conversation: A Documentary on a Taboo Subject. Produced by Michael Bern Hagen. Directed by Terry Kaldhusdal. Burning Hay Wagon Productions, 2011.

Dilbeck, M. The Response Ability Project: A Call for Courage. http://www.mikedilbeck.com/.

Edwards, Keith E. "Aspiring Social Justice Ally Identity Development: A Conceptual Model." *NASPA Journal* 43, no. 4 (2007). doi:10.2202/0027-6014.1722.

Ertel, Chris, and Lisa Kay Solomon. *Moments of Impact: How to Design Strategic Conversations That Accelerate Change.* New York: Simon & Schuster, 2014.

Fabiano, Patricia M., H. Wesley Perkins, Alan Berkowitz, Jeff Linkenbach, and Christopher Stark. "Engaging Men as Social Justice Allies in Ending Violence Against Women: Evidence for a Social Norms Approach." *Journal of American College Health* 52, no. 3 (2003): 105–12. doi:10.1080/07448480309595732.

Fricker, Miranda. *Epistemic Injustice: Power and the Ethics of Knowing*. Oxford: Oxford University Press, 2007.

Freire, Paulo. *Pedagogy of the Oppressed*. New York: Continuum, 2000.

Gandhi, and Mahadev H. Desai. *Gandhi, an Autobiography: The Story of My Experiments with Truth*. Boston: Beacon Press, 1957.

Gide, André. *Autumn Leaves*. New York: Philosophical Library, 2007.

Goodman, Diane J. "Motivating People from Privileged Groups to Support Social Justice." *Teachers College Record* 102, no. 6 (2000): 1061-085. doi:10.1111/0161-4681.00092.

Guest, Laurie. *Wrapped in Stillness: A Personal Retreat Guide*. Rolling Meadows, IL: WindyCityPub, 2013.

Harro, B. *The Cycle of Socialization* in Adams, Maurianne, W. J. Blumenfield, R. Castaneda, H. L. Hackman, M. LP, and X. Zuniga, eds. *Readings for Diversity and Social Justice: An Anthology on Racism, Anti-Semitism, Sexism, Heterosexism, Ableism and Classism*. New York: Routledge, 2000.

Heen, Sheila, Douglas Stone, and Bruce Patton. *Difficult Conversations: How to Discuss What Matters Most*. New York, NY: Penguin Books, 2000.

Helms, Janet E. *A Race Is a Nice Thing to Have: A Guide to Being a White Person or Understanding the White Persons in Your Life*. Topeka: Content Communications, 1992.

Helms, Janet E. *An Update of Helms' White and People of Color Racial Identity Models* in Ponterotto, Joseph G., J. Manuel Casas, Lisa A. Suzuki, and Charlene M. Alexander, eds. *Handbook of Multicultural Counseling*. Thousand Oaks, CA: Sage Publications, 1995.

Hollins, Caprice D., and Ilsa M. Govan. *Diversity, Equity, and Inclusion: Strategies for Facilitating Conversations on Race*. Lanham: Rowman & Littlefield, 2015.

hooks, bell. *Teaching to Transgress: Education as the Practice of Freedom*. New York: Routledge, 1994.

Huffington, Arianna Stassinopoulos. *Thrive: The Third Metric to Redefining Success and Creating a Life of Well-Being, Wisdom, and Wonder*. New York: Harmony Books, 2014.

INCITE! *Color of Violence: The INCITE! Anthology*. Cambridge, MA: South End Press, 2006.

Irving, Debby. *Waking Up White: And Finding Myself in the Story of Race*. Cambridge, MA: Elephant Room Press, 2014.

James, William. *On Vital Reserves: The Energies of Men; The Gospel of Relaxation.* New York: H. Holt, 1911.

Jealous, Ann Todd, and Caroline T. Haskell, eds. *Combined Destinies: Whites Sharing Grief about Racism.* Washington, D.C.: Potomac Books, 2013.

Johnson, Allan G. *Privilege, Power, and Difference.* Boston, MA: McGraw-Hill, 2006.

Jones, Charisse, and Kumea Shorter-Gooden. *Shifting: The Double Lives of Black Women in America.* New York: HarperCollins, 2003.

Katz, Judy H. *White Awareness: Handbook for Anti-racism Training.* Norman: University of Oklahoma Press, 1978.

Kegan, Robert. *In Over Our Heads: The Mental Demands of Modern Life.* Cambridge, MA: Harvard University Press, 1994.

Kendall, Frances E. *Understanding White Privilege: Creating Pathways to Authentic Relationships across Race.* New York: Routledge, 2006.

Sun Kim, Christine. "The Enchanting Music of Sign Language." TED Talks. August 2015. http://www.ted.com/talks/ christine_sun_kim_the_enchanting_music_of_sign_language.

Kivel, Paul. "Social Service, or Social Change?" Paul Kivel: Educator, Writer, Activist. Accessed November 14, 2016. http://paulkivel .com/resource/social-service-or-social-change.

Komives, Susan R., Julie E. Owen, Susan D. Longerbeam, Felicia C. Mainella, and Laura Osteen. "Developing a Leadership Identity: A Grounded Theory." *Journal of College Student Development* 46, no. 6 (2005): 593-611. doi:10.1353/csd.2005.0061.

Kotecki, Jason W. *Penguins Can't Fly: +39 Other Rules That Don't Exist.* New York: St. Martin's Griffin, 2015.

Linker, Maureen. *Intellectual Empathy: Critical Thinking for Social Justice.* Ann Arbor: University of Michigan Press, 2015.

Loeb, Paul Rogat. *Soul of a Citizen: Living with Conviction in Challenging Times.* New York: St. Martin's Griffin, 2010.

Mackey, John, and Rajendra Sisodia. *Conscious Capitalism: Liberating the Heroic Spirit of Business.* Boston, MA: Harvard Business Review Press, 2013.

Mattson, Matthew G., Jessica Gendron Williams, and Joshua A. Orendi. *Social Excellence: We Dare You.* Carmel, IN: Phired Up Productions, 2011.

McEwen, M. "New Perspective on Identity Development" in Komives, Susan R., and Dudley Woodard. *Student Services: A Handbook for the Profession*. San Francisco: Jossey-Bass, 2003.

McIntosh, Peggy. *White Privilege and Male Privilege: A Personal Account of Coming to See Correspondences through Work in Women's Studies*. Wellesley, MA: Wellesley College, Center for Research on Women, 1988

Nash, Robert J., Richard Greggory. Johnson, and Michele C. Murray. *Teaching College Students Communication Strategies for Effective Social Justice Advocacy*. New York: Peter Lang, 2012.

Northwest Earth Institute. "Seeing Systems: Peace, Justice, & Sustainability." Online discussion course, Northwest Earth Institute, 2014. www.nwei.org.

Patterson, Kerry, J. Grenny, R. McMillan, and A. Switzler. *Crucial Conversations: Tools for Talking When Stakes Are High*. 2nd ed. New York: McGraw-Hill, 2012.

Putnam, Robert D. *Bowling Alone: The Collapse and Revival of American Community*. New York: Simon & Schuster, 2000.

Reason, Robert D., Ellen M. Broido, T. L. Davis, and N. J. Evans, eds. *Developing Social Justice Allies, Number 110*. San Francisco: Jossey-Bass, 2005.

Reddy, Maureen T. *Everyday Acts against Racism: Raising Children in a Multiracial World*. Seattle, WA: Seal Press, 1996.

Rhoads, Robert, and M. A. Black. "Student Affairs Practitioners as Transformative Educators: Advancing a Critical Cultural Perspective." *Journal of College Student Development* 36, no. 5 (January 1995): 413–21.

Rivers, Dennis, Gene Knudsen Hoffman, Leah Green, and Cynthia Monroe. *The Seven Challenges Workbook: A Guide to Cooperative Communication Skills for Success at Home and at Work*. Berkeley, CA: Human Development Books, 2007.

Roberts, Dennis C. *Deeper Learning in Leadership: Helping College Students Find the Potential Within*. San Francisco: Jossey-Bass, 2007.

Scott, Susan. *Fierce Conversations: Achieving Success at Work & in Life, One Conversation at a Time*. New York, NY: Berkley Books, 2004.

Senge, Peter M., C. Roberts, R. B. Ross, B. J. Smith, and A. Kleiner. *The Fifth Discipline Fieldbook: Strategies and Tools for Building a Learning Organization*. New York: Currency, Doubleday, 1994.

Singleton, Glenn E., and Curtis Linton. *Courageous Conversations about Race: A Field Guide for Achieving Equity in Schools.* Thousand Oaks, CA: Corwin Press, 2006.

Sue, Derald Wing. *Microaggressions in Everyday Life: Race, Gender, and Sexual Orientation.* Hoboken, NJ: Wiley, 2010.

Tatum, Beverly. "Talking about Race, Learning about Racism: The Application of Racial Identity Development Theory in the Classroom." *Harvard Educational Review* 62, no. 1 (1992): 1-25. doi:10.17763/haer.62.1.146k5v980r703023.

Tatum, Beverly. *"Why Are All the Black Kids Sitting Together in the Cafeteria?": And Other Conversations about Race.* New York: Basic Books, 2003.

Theoharis, Jeanne. *The Rebellious Life of Mrs. Rosa Parks.* Boston: Beacon Press, 2013.

Tochluk, Shelly. *Witnessing Whiteness: The Need to Talk about Race and How to Do It.* Lanham, MD: Rowman & Littlefield Education, 2010.

Turkle, Sherry. *Alone Together: Why We Expect More from Technology and Less from Each Other.* New York: Basic Books, 2011.

Washington, J., "Becoming an Ally" in Evans, Nancy J., and Vernon A. Wall, eds. *Beyond Tolerance: Gays, Lesbians, and Bisexuals on Campus.* Alexandria, VA: American College Personnel Association, 1991.

White, Augustus A., and David Chanoff. *Seeing Patients: Unconscious Bias in Health Care.* Cambridge, MA: Harvard University Press, 2011.

Wise, Tim J. *White Like Me: Reflections on Race from a Privileged Son.* Brooklyn, NY: Soft Skull Press, 2008.

Wijeyesinghe, Charmaine, and Bailey W. Jackson, eds. *New Perspectives on Racial Identity Development: A Theoretical and Practical Anthology.* New York: New York University Press, 2001.

Yankelovich, Daniel. *The Magic of Dialogue: Transforming Conflict into Cooperation.* New York: Simon & Schuster, 1999 in Beyond War Study Series. http://beyondwarnw.org.

Yoshino, Kenji, and Christie Smith. "Fear of Being Different Stifles Talent." *Harvard Business Review.* March 31, 2014. https://hbr.org/2014/03/fear-of-being-different-stifles-talent.

Zander, Rosamund Stone, and Benjamin Zander. *The Art of Possibility: Transforming Professional and Personal Life.* Camberwell, Vic.: Penguin, 2002.

ACKNOWLEDGMENTS

October 27, 2015, the best teacher I ever had passed away. Dr. James M. Jennings saw me before I saw me. As a secondary education major at Hendrix College, I took my first course with Dr. Jennings in 1994. My mother had passed away at the beginning of my sophomore year, and I had stayed home to try to glue my family together. It didn't work, so I left and returned to campus in 1994. Dr. Jennings drew the short straw and was assigned as my advisor.

I was angry, lost, pained, numb, and hurting. Dr. Jennings—no matter the condition I was in when I showed up, often late and after many no-shows—held one-on-one advisor sessions where I was allowed just to "be." Slowly, being me helped me heal, find direction, and eventually discover the inequities in education and a primer to an understanding of power and privilege.

I wouldn't be the person I am today without his soft chuckle, directed questions, suggested readings, and complete and total acceptance.

A handful of years later, I returned to my undergraduate institution to speak to the students in the very classroom where I had attended my first class with Dr. Jennings. It was in this classroom where I was introduced to *Before the Mayflower: A Brief History of Black America* by Lerone Bennett. I now see that the Good Enough Now model started with Dr. Jennings. As I unlearned the history I had been taught in high school and relearned the truth about the world, my *head* began to gather new information and made me want to take *action* and be a better history teacher. This exposure paired with my first real mentor and tapped my *heart* to impact as many people as possible with the truth of systems of oppression. Dr. Jennings sat in my audience while I spoke of the rudimentary beginning of the content of this book and took notes. He took notes about my message!

Several years after graduation, I was doing some research and came upon an article that Dr. Jennings had written. I debated calling him, questioned whether he would remember me, felt silly, and reached out anyway. He seemed to be in his office all the time, and like clockwork he answered the phone. We talked for hours about the state of education in our country. He was a good teacher because he was always learning. I try to do the same.

Dr. Jennings was teaching a class when he said he was feeling overheated. He left his classroom and returned to his office, where he passed away. In the time since, students, colleagues, friends, and family have shared what a difference he made in individual lives and across education in the Delta of Arkansas. He didn't fix the education crisis in our country. He did, however, make a difference.

> **The concept of Good Enough Now is exactly this—trying instead of winning.**

We, as humanity, are responsible for who we are and how we show up (and don't), and it is good and useful. Sure, there may be improvements, edits, or learning, that need to occur, but fundamentally, I believe we are good. Our own self-limiting talk, excuses, fears, and the like, prevent us from building, moving, growing, and living. What if we are enough right now? I believe we must do the best we can with what we have even if it is only some of the time. Our time is limited. Typically, we don't know how long we have. With this understanding, we can become self-aware enough to accept our own good, bad, and ugly, so to speak, and use our own lived experiences to try.

Now is the time to get started.

If you are interested in supporting the Dr. James Jennings Scholarship Fund, visit:

https://www.hendrix.edu/giving/

or send a contribution to:

Hendrix College
ATTN: Rev. J. Wayne Clark
Associate Vice President of Development &
Dean of the Chapel
1600 Washington Avenue
Conway, Arkansas 72032

For inquiries call (501) 450-1223 or e-mail Clark@Hendrix.edu.

GLOSSARY

Ally
Being someone that others turn to that listens and makes educated referrals.

Antidote
Something you take or do to counteract a problem, mistake, or undesirable situation so we can be good enough now.

Assumptions
Guessing information about someone or something else based on one's own expectations and experiences and not factual information derived from a conversation.

Behavioral Patterns
Acting or reacting to similar situations in similar manners over a period of time.

Bystander Behavior
When someone observes something that should be interrupted or stopped and we do nothing.

Cisgender	Cis is a Latin prefix meaning congruent. In the case of one's gender, if we identify with the gender that we were labeled as at birth, as well as how we were raised, we are cisgender and have cisgender privilege. Often we are referred to as a cisman or ciswoman.
Compassionate Exhaustion	When we care so much about a particular cause that we work until we are burnt out and can no longer work.
Conscious Behavioral Patterns	Being fully aware of how we are acting or reacting to similar situations in similar manners over a period of time.
Conscious Bias	Being fully aware of how we have positive or negative assumptions about someone or something.
crucible moments	Positive or negative moments in our lives that occur and when we are able to look back on them, we know they were life-changing moments in our own development as a person.
Differently Right	Being able to see someone, something, or even a part of yourself that is frustrating as something that is powerful and/or necessary even for a short window of time.
Dominant Identities	Often viewed as privileged statuses or labels in our society. These identities are extended a sense of power that other identities are not. (White, Man, Upper-Class, Christian, Able-Bodied, Citizen, Heterosexual, etc.)
Enough	What is needed to keep trying to try. The belief that doing the best we can with what we have some of the time is better than nothing.
Gas Pedal	Typically fueled by our third element, we can accelerate or slow way down with excuses when confronting something uncomfortable or new.
"Go Around" Idea	Instead of being stuck, we can make a decision to utilize our third place and like a gas pedal, push through an excuse pattern or emotional response and keep trying to try.

Holding Space — Either for one's own development and/or for others', holding space is intentionally creating an opportunity for a learning moment, conversation, or personal interaction to occur fully and uninterrupted.

Impact — Intentional or not, the way our behaviors, words, and/or reactions land on someone else. We are responsible for our impact.

Inside Voice — When we talk to ourselves and make judgments and assumptions to feel safe and prepared. These are often unheard by others but others see the outcome.

Intent — What we genuinely mean to say or do in response to someone or something.

Internalized Oppression — The self belief that because of an identity or experience we have had, we are less than or deserving of less than those different than us.

Intersection of Identities — Pulling from Kimberlé Crenshaw's work, we have more than one identity and it is at the complicated intersection of these identities that we need to hold for ourself and for others when looking at our collective identities and experiences.

Judgments — A decision that often informs our biases, prejudices, and response behaviors. We make judgments to feel safe and prepared. These judgments also often register as facts or the truth to us and often are inaccurate.

Kryptonite — The one element that hurt Superman was Kryptonite and our excuse patterns are the same way. Our third variable can act as a gas pedal and accelerate us through a tough situation or we can get stuck and falter.

Leaving Room for Edits — This is the concept of making judgments to feel safe and prepared, but realizing they might not be accurate. We then must actively seek more accurate information and update our assumptions.

Lens
The collection of identities and experiences that we interpret the world through act as a kind of glasses both improving and impairing our vision.

Lived Experiences
The collection of memories, crucible moments, and happenings that inform the stories from those around us and in our own lives that we use to share with others.

Microagression
Often seen as small things that have a larger impact on others. A mispronounced name due to an unfamiliarity with the name itself may seem small, but time and time again can accumulate into a powerfully negative experience. It is important to keep trying to try to lessen the accumulation of negative experiences of others.

Negative Bias
A judgment or assumption about someone or something, a place or event, or behavior that you looked down upon. Sometimes we can identify why and sometimes we cannot.

Negative Explicit Bias
Intentionally employing a negative judgment to inform a response.

Negative Implicit Bias
Unintentionally employing a negative judgment to inform a response.

Party of-One Work
Self-reflection work that takes responsibility for who and how we individually show up in the world.

Personal Triggers
Patterns of events, behaviors, words, or situations that routinely result in a similar, often emotional response that may or may not be related to the individual circumstances but one's cumulative lived experiences.

Pile up
Pulling from Maura Cullen's work, the accumulation of similar experiences that often result in a larger response than each individual experience would garner.

Positive Bias
A judgment or assumption about someone or something, a place or event, or behavior that you looked up to or gave an advantage.

Positive Explicit Bias	Intentionally employing a positive judgment to inform a response.
Positive Implicit Bias	Unintentionally employing a positive judgment to inform a response.
Radical Amazement	The ability to continue to be self-motivated when working with people that equally support a similar cause.
(Re)claiming Responsibility	We are responsible for who and how we show up in the world. For some, we must start with claiming our own behavior patterns and for others, we need to continue to do this and keep repeating the process.
Righter	No one likes to admit they are wrong, so this is about getting more accurate.
Self-Work	Becoming more self-aware or conscious of one's self and our own behavior patterns—the good, bad, ugly and awesome.
Subordinated Identities	The labels and lived experiences that are not empowered by our culture or seen by others as advantages. These identities or experiences often lead to being silenced or marginalized, consciously and unconsciously, by others from more privileged groups.
The Observer or Third Party	This person isn't intended to be a part of the conversation but observes it, overhears it, or learns about it from someone else.
The Receiver	Is the person that is being communicated with.
The Sender	Is the person with the message for the Receiver.
The Third Party or Observer	This person isn't intended to be a part of the conversation but observes it, overhears it, or learns about it from someone else.
Them	The collective members of a group that we think don't belong.

Third Rail   Of the three elements, the one that we typically respond from the least often. The third rail fuels our excuse patterns and can push us into being unstoppable.

Trigger Roots   The lived experiences that develop into trigger patterns have roots fueled by our life identities. We are responsible for the roots of our personal triggers.

Try to Keep Trying   The power of being *enough* is that we can make an attempt, and whether we fail or succeed, we can learn from it and make another attempt again.

Us   The collective members of a group to which we do belong.

Unconscious Behavioral Patterns   Not being fully aware of how we are acting or reacting to similar situations in similar manners over a period of time, yet still behaving in patterns that others experience.

Unconscious Bias   Not being fully aware of how we have positive or negative assumptions about someone or something, yet doing it anyway.

Unicorn Points   Redeemable nowhere, with no commercial value, but still very exciting to receive.

Vaccine   When conscious of our behavioral patterns, we can keep the ones we like and work to develop habits that better suit our desired way of being. Unlike an antidote, this preemptive measure creates desired outcomes before there is a problem, mistake, or undesirable situation allowing us to be good enough now.

TWEETABLES

@jesspettitt #goodenoughnow

The concept of Good Enough Now is exactly this—trying instead of winning.

We are Good Enough Now.

"Become the imitable thing." —WILLIAM JAMES

Never quit trying to try.

"Conscience makes cowards of us all." —WILLIAM JAMES

"The best time to plant a tree is twenty years ago. The second best time is now." —CHINESE PROVERB

"Ego says, 'Once everything falls into place, I'll feel peace.' Spirit says, 'Find your peace, and then everything will fall into place.'" —MARIANNE WILLIAMSON

"I put up with whatever cost I have to put up with, because the cost of not doing the work is greater." —TIM WISE

Society will change for the better when we individually do our own work.

"When you're accustomed to privilege, equality feels like oppression." —AFRO PUNK MEME

Holding space for others matters.

Feeling a part of the problem is how I got out of my own way and started making and seeing real change in my own life.

Leaving space for someone else to be good enough is revolutionary.

We must cross the streams, do something different, to get a different result.

Practice...breathe...reflect...learn...repeat.

"Authenticity is not something you have; it is something you choose." —SHEILA HEEN, DOUGLAS STONE, AND BRUCE PATTON

"Every sentence has a history." —KERRY PATTERSON

"Adults are weird and worry instead of wonder."

Listen to others as if they are wise.

"I think courage is the ability to tell your story. I've heard so many stories in my life that I know I'm not alone. Everyone has a struggle." —BRENÉ BROWN

"Let us not cease to love the truth even when it is unfavorable to us." —ANDRÉ GIDE

My identity is about being resilient and inspiring others to do the same. That is success.

"Do I not destroy my enemies when I make them my friends?" —ABRAHAM LINCOLN

"It is better to be hated for what you are than to be loved for what you are not." —ANDRÉ GIDE, Autumn Leaves

We succeed or learn.

Indeed, acting yourself to a new way of thinking is easier than thinking your way to a new way of acting.

What have I learned about myself?

"The role of the artist is exactly the same as the role of the lover. If I love you, I have to make you conscious of the things you don't see." —JAMES BALDWIN

We are all complicated. If we can embrace intention and impact as truths that often are coming from different places, we can truly begin to listen to each other and connect.

It is imperative to understand that to be enough is to reflect on one's own lived experiences and determine our habitual behavioral patterns.

Raising a fist or awareness, marching in the streets, striking a picket line, kneeling on the sidelines, staying seated are all responses that matter.

Doing something uncomfortable is where growth, change, and connection can take place.

We are responsible for the accuracy of our stories.

We present a story about ourselves to others.

As you notice response and behavioral patterns in others and in yourself, it is important to not make meaning of these patterns and just notice them for what they are.

One must speak with the oppressed without speaking for the oppressed.

What are your turning points? What are your crucible moments?

If you pick out the most frustrating person in your life (which might be you), can you give enough space for complications that you didn't expect?

We can do this. We are good enough now. I promise.

"We are the experts we have been waiting for." —BRENDON BURCHARD

"We are the ones we have been waiting for." —HOPI PROPHECY

When you add up all of the "us" groups and "me" groups out there—you are left with "we."

The problem is that your "them" isn't absolute. Someone in the "them" group sees you as their "them." Real change doesn't lie outside of us.

To be clear, there is a difference between discomfort and a lack of safety.

Head, Heart, and Action are at our disposal if not already automatically at play when we engage in a situation, conversation, or opportunity to make a connection.

To truly reclaim responsibility for our own responses and behavior patterns, we have to start with some structure.

Take notice.

This is super simple, but it isn't easy.

Taking responsibility for who and how we are is our responsibility.

Releasing something into the world for judgments is exhilarating and terrifying until it becomes comfortable and a habit.

What would happen if we just tried anyway?

We must connect for us to feel like we matter.

Imagine how much more productive, innovative, curious, generous, and authentic we would be if we didn't feel the pressure to "cover."

FREEBIES

www.GoodEnoughNow.com/Freebies

- Individual workbooks
- Self-assessment
- Download app now on Android and iTunes called:

JESSICA PETTIT

ABOUT JESSICA PETTITT

It is through Jessica's work as a college administrator in student affairs in South Carolina, Oregon, New York, Arizona, and California that she realized her love for the conversations across difference. As a returned Peace Corps volunteer, Social Justice Training Institute alumna, and a Certified Speaking Professional, Jessica has taken the typical diversity talks to the next level of social justice conversations, examining privilege, oppression, entitlement, and our collective responsibility to make change while connecting difficult topics with employee retention, crisis management, and increasing innovation and profits.

Referred to as the "Margaret Cho" of diversity trainers, Jessica blends politics, humor, identity, and local flair with big-city passion and energy through direct, individualized, and interactive conversations. Her workshops, seminars, and keynotes don't just leave participants invigorated, but inspired and motivated to follow through with action to create change. Having traveled and lived in a variety of communities and environments all over the world while also engaging with education as a student, teacher, administrator, and active community member, Jessica uses her take on life to lead participants through a safe but confrontational process of examination, self-reflection, and open dialogue that is as challenging as it is rewarding.

Responses to Jessica's programs are overwhelmingly positive and include comments ranging from, "This was awful—I never had to think so hard while laughing!" to "I can't believe my boss brought her—thanks for actually treating us like adults," to "She answered all of my questions knowledgeably and without making me feel dumb for asking."

With her attention now turning to larger associations and corporate leadership, Jessica is pulling from the past fifteen years of direct experience to lead teams to try, instead of avoiding a stretch. It is in this trying that clients uncover a deeper sense of belonging, discover resourceful collaboration opportunities, and reignite their creativity and innovative ideation. Learning, feeling, and being Good Enough Now allows for teams to do the best they can with what they have and persist long into the future no matter the crisis, topic, or challenge.

Graduating from the University of South Carolina with an M.Ed. in Higher Education Administration with an emphasis in Crisis Management, Jessica pulls together lessons from teaching History and English in the classroom, as well as those from the stand-up comedy stages of New York City, to bring real and actionable results to meeting rooms and board tables. She is well published, including multiple DVD and online training courses, curriculum guides, and a book that makes the abstract actionable.

To learn more about bringing Jessica to your next event, retreat, or the like, visit www.goodenoughnow.com.

ENDORSEMENTS

I had the honor of experiencing *Good Enough Now* in its fledgling state. After consuming it voraciously, I immediately reread it and followed every exercise. The content is immersive and relatable, and I was able to instantly apply it in my own life. I noticed a shift in how I communicate; specifically how I listen and truly hear others. Being aware of the concepts in this book has affected how I show up in the world in my various roles. The weighty work that this book challenges the reader to do is coded in the author's humor and voice, making it enjoyable and seamless. It was a fun and crucial experience. I am good enough now.

MEGAN BISSELL, Greeley, CO

Jessica Pettitt is a force of nature...inspiring and teaching us with inclusive leadership of how to exceed the expectations we have for ourselves and allowing us to show up with our strengths, supporting others and creating teams members that encourage making for stronger influence in the workplace and in our communities. The comprehensive way Jessica breaks things down, I can see a clear path to work purposefully and be more than good enough now.

CONNIE PHIEFF, Phieff Group

Over the years, I've taught hundreds of college students who are struggling to interact with each other and understand themselves. I can say without a doubt that *Good Enough Now* is exactly what our world needs at this moment and Jess is exactly the right person to deliver this message. *Good Enough Now* offers a fresh perspective filled with practical application.

—JOSH PACKARD, PH.D., Associate Professor of Sociology, University of Northern Colorado